We Are Not Alone

How ECK Masters Guide
Our Spiritual Lives Today

We Are Not Alone

How ECK Masters Guide
Our Spiritual Lives Today

Robert Marsh

ECKANKAR
Minneapolis, MN

We Are Not Alone: How ECK Masters
Guide Our Spiritual Lives Today

Copyright © 1994 Robert Marsh

Printed in U.S.A.

Edited by Joan Klemp
Anthony Moore
Mary Carroll Moore

Cover design by Lois Stanfield
Cover illustration concept by Sandro Pasetto
Cover illustration by Shirley Cean Young

Library of Congress Cataloging-in-Publication Data

Marsh, Robert, 1955–
    We are not alone : how Eck masters guide our spiritual
lives today / Robert Marsh.
        p. cm.
      ISBN 1-57043-062-4 : $11.00
      1. Eckankar (Organization)—Doctrines. 2. Marsh, Robert,
1955– —Religion. 3. Eck masters. 4. Eckists. I. Title.
BP605.E3M37 1994
299' .93—dc20   94–9348
                                                      CIP

Contents

Chapter Six: The Swans of God

Chapter Seven: Secret Teachings

Chapter Eight: The Golden Child

Chapter Nine: Spiritual Marriage

Chapter Ten: The Great Wall

Chapter Eleven: Opening the Gate

Chapter Twelve: Wee Two, We Four

Introduction

When I was a child, I wondered if adults were keeping valuable information from me. Birthdays became important because I half expected with each advancing year to be allowed to share the true wisdom with my elders. But, of course, this never happened.

The true wisdom in my life came from my guardian angel. At two, I would sing to him in my crib, and from age six I'd often go alone to the front room after school and sit with this familiar presence who listened to me. When I was young, I knew him by the name Ubi Quando. I was later to recognize him as the ECK Master Fubbi Quantz.

It seemed easy to think of him as an angel, but I never thought of him as a Catholic angel. I didn't see life the way my parents saw it, and the religion I grew up in did not meet my spiritual needs. Fubbi asked me to be patient with my parents and teachers, to follow their guidance until I was older.

My experiences with Fubbi Quantz and other Vairagi Masters of ECKANKAR convinced me that we are not alone in the universe. These beings gave me guidance through my growing-up years, and then

I found the teachings of ECKANKAR in 1975. This book is the story of my journey to the present. It is one person's approach to God, nothing more.

It's my sincere hope that these stories will assist others in addressing their own spiritual questions. I try to identify basic principles which apply universally and show how an understanding of them can quietly improve one's spiritual life.

There are no goals more lofty, more worthy of our total effort and aspiration, than Self-Realization and God-Realization in this lifetime. My story may help someone take a step further on that path and realize the immense help that is available to each Soul. In truth, we are not alone.

Chapter One

Golden Lifetime

1. Singing

At the age of two, I would lie awake in bed at night and stare at the ceiling. A silent question would form: Why had I been placed here on earth again?

I felt trapped, sadly removed from a glorious source of past happiness which I couldn't quite recall. I was greatly troubled by the knowledge that I couldn't leave this world for many years, until I was old enough to die.

When the tension got too great, I'd stand up in my high-railed crib and begin to sing, rocking the crib from side to side. My parents could hear this nightly concert from the room below. Sometimes in the morning they wouldn't be able to get the door open. The crib would inch across the room as I rocked it, often blocking the door.

Curiously, I could remember always singing *to* someone. I thought of this being as my guardian angel.

*   *   *

By the time I started school, this guardian angel's presence had become very familiar. Once a week I'd lie on the couch in the front room and review my life with him, what had happened in school and at home. Basically, I didn't see life the way my parents saw it, and it was a great relief to me to have someone to talk to. There was no one else I could turn to. Who would understand?

This Master was very kind and listened carefully. At that time it seemed easiest to think of him as an angel, but I never imagined him to be a Catholic angel, although that was the faith practiced by my parents. He seemed to be outside the rituals of Catholicism, in a way which comforted me.

This Master always asked me to be patient with my parents and teachers. He told me to follow their guidance until I was older. This was never what I wanted to hear, but he gave much the same advice every time we talked. He reminded me that even though I knew the information and supposed truths given to me by my elders were defective, I must be patient and abide by them until I could make my own decisions—and live by them.

In the early years of my life between ages six and eleven, I often wondered why I had to live at all. I found it very difficult to will myself into conforming with society. I loved people, but at the same time I felt as though I dwelled on the periphery of life. The Catholic religion had interesting ideas about God and the world, but they were full of contradictions. None of them brought me any deep satisfaction.

This inner struggle was unexpectedly resolved at age eleven.

2. Golden Lifetime

When I was eleven years old, I was suddenly struck down by a severe attack of asthma. I had no prior history of the disease.

Within days I became gravely ill, and my parents checked me into a hospital. Breathing became a painful struggle, and my strength was being depleted very quickly. One evening the doctor took my mother aside and told her that I could possibly die before morning.

That night I stood by in a tranquil state, watching my body heave and gasp for breath. It looked as if the end had finally come. But I felt no fear. I was actually quite content to die. After all, my life had not made much sense to me so far. Perhaps I would be able to go back to that place of happiness, of light and love, that I barely remembered.

Just then, at the corner of my inner vision, I saw the familiar form of my guardian angel. He radiated an atmosphere of love. A soft, sweet light began to surround me, and in silent language we communicated.

"Do you really want to pass over, Robert?" he asked me, smiling with great love.

As he said these words, it suddenly occurred to me that I had the choice of whether to live or die. And at that same moment, I sensed for the first time the profound spiritual value of life here on earth. Awash in the love of this Master and greatly reassured about living, I felt I would be able to find happiness here.

"I'll stay!" I replied silently.

My health took a turn for the better that night, and I made a speedy recovery. Ten days later I was discharged from the hospital and taken home.

It was a paradox to me that such a healing—one that allowed me to live here fully rather than long for death—came as a result of a near-fatal illness. The conflict of being born into this alien world can be a great burden, especially for a child. A tension is created that causes endless agitation and spiritual upset.

My healing came because of the encouragement I felt from my invisible Master, who had given me a silent promise that I would be able to reach the happiness I sought. It was a promise that this lifetime would be the most important one I had ever lived, and that I owed it to myself to make it a golden one.

3. Ghosts

I was still a young child when my parents told me that we would soon be moving to a new home. It had been occupied by the local Catholic curates.

The atmosphere of our new home was strangely uncomfortable to me. I got along fine for about a year, and then the trouble started.

A host of resident entities in that house began to plague me. Getting to sleep each night became a journey through hell. There was nothing my parents could do to console me. Prayer didn't work; I called on Jesus and the saints to no avail.

This constant psychic harassment was torture. I dreaded bedtime. Being only six, I wasn't very skilled at articulating my problem. Facing these creatures nightly was becoming an ordeal. One elderly lady in particular regarded certain rooms as her own. While housekeeper to the priests who had lived there, she'd passed away in one of the back bedrooms and now refused to leave.

One night several months after this inner turmoil began, I was resting with my eyes closed when something very special happened. A glowing white image appeared quietly in my inner vision. Standing calmly before me, this being spoke soothing words, inviting me to trust completely in him and let go of all care. He conveyed this message telepathically, much as my guardian angel and I communicated.

With a gentle, reassuring smile, he told me to think of him as my spiritual father. He was emphatic on this point. He said that if I maintained this inner bond of trust, I would enjoy his complete protection. The entities would become powerless to harm me.

Soothing waves of love filled the room, dispelling all tension. I sensed that the entities had vanished. Then this dignified being bade me goodnight and faded from my vision. I would not see him again.

To insure that I developed this inner bond of trust, my guardian angel appeared for two nights after this and imparted the same loving message.

And they were right: the entities never bothered me again.

4. Three Memories

When I was five years old, I loved singing with my classmates in school. The little organ the teacher played made a lovely sound. As she played, she would adjust the brightly colored stops, her sweet melodies charming our tiny hearts. We joined in with whatever words we could remember.

One song in particular brought a flood of old and forgotten memories. A Scottish ballad, "Westering Home," caused emotions to well up from deep inside me, calling to me like a tender voice from behind high walls. I often burst into tears when the teacher played this song. I could never explain why.

Even as children, many of us glimpse past lives, and these memories can be deeply moving. In this instance I was remembering two lifetimes just gone, one in the United States and one in Ireland.

* * *

While still a small boy, I would practice certain physical exercises on the floor of my room. Though the room was unheated, even on cold winter evenings, I never found it necessary to wear any clothing. My body seemed to generate enough heat on its

9

own. I couldn't figure it out, but I knew the ability to keep warm was related in some way to the exercises.

The exercises involved holding certain postures for a period of time. This continued for about three years, at which time I lost interest in the postures I had practiced.

It was only in later years, when I learned about yoga and its various postures, that I recognized my exercises. The yogic phase in my childhood was a carryover from certain Eastern past lives.

*   *   *

When I was eleven, a young American boy came to live in our town. He brought with him sets of sport cards. I collected many sport cards during those years—soccer, racing, and airplane heroes—but none held my interest like American baseball. Yet I knew absolutely nothing about the game because it was not even played in my country.

At the time this was very puzzling. Neither the game nor the personalities on the cards were the least bit familiar to me, so why this strong attraction?

I didn't realize it then, but my incarnation just prior to this one was in North Carolina. Though I had died young, at eighteen, I had had a love for baseball. So when I saw those cards again, I felt irresistibly attracted to them.

5. Rain

Lying in bed at night, I'd carry out my usual review of the day, conversing with my inner guardian. While looking up at the ceiling, I'd reflect in a neutral, unhurried way on the string of events that had made up my day. Often I'd hear rain falling outside while I did this.

This happened so often that I got curious about the rain. Why did it always fall when I went into this quiet, neutral state of mind?

It always sounded the same too. Surely the rain should vary in its intensity from time to time.

One night, overcome with curiosity, I decided to investigate. I sat up in bed, and the sound of the rain suddenly stopped. I walked over to the window, opened it, and placed my hand on the sill. It was dry. I went outside into the garden in my pajamas; the grass was dry beneath my bare feet.

Yet when I climbed back into bed and resumed my reverie, the sound of the rain started again. This is how I became familiar as a child with one of the pure, uplifting sounds of the Holy Spirit. The rain I was hearing was not the kind that wet the grass and made flowers bloom; it was the Sound of God.

11

6. The Black Dog

One lovely bright Saturday in March, I set off to visit a friend. Absorbed in the beauty of the morning, I forgot completely about repeated warnings never to arrive by the rear of the house. It was only after I had entered the yard and approached the back door that I heard a deep growl from behind me.

The black dog at this house was so savage that he had to be confined to the yard at all times.

I stood frozen on the doorstep; there was no retreat. He blocked my exit. By the look in his eye, I knew the huge black brute was about to sink his teeth into my tender flesh.

My heart began to pound. I told myself not to panic, and a strange calm came over me. An inner voice said clearly, "Keep your back to the door." I only understood the reason for this after the dog pounced. I knew if the dog succeeded in getting me to the ground, I was finished. But the door supported my body, and the impact failed to knock me down.

"Put your hand near his mouth!" commanded the inner voice.

This seemed crazy. The black dog was snarling and growling, teeth bared. But I did as the silent voice had instructed. As soon as I put my hand to the dog's mouth, the voice told me to shove my hand down the dog's throat as far as I could.

"Hold his neck firm against your body with your other arm!" came next. Only now did any of this make sense. The dog was powerless to close his jaws; neither could he pull himself free, since I gripped his neck tightly to my chest. The door supported me from behind, and I had the dog off balance, unable to knock me over with his great weight.

But I could feel my strength failing. There was nothing I could do to subdue the huge animal, and he would soon overpower me. At that moment the last instruction came, "Kick the door with your heel!"

I realized this would work. It was the only movement I could make and still keep my balance. At the sound my friend's father hurried out and managed to drag the dog off. He was just in time. I was unhurt; not a scratch. The family thought it was a miracle.

Oddly enough the experience didn't upset me. I felt quietly delighted by the protection I had received. But I heard nothing from the voice until a similar incident began at school later that year.

7. The Boxing Match

While playing cops and robbers one morning before class, one boy was accidentally knocked to the ground. Another unintentionally stepped on his head. The boy slowly picked himself up, livid with rage, looking for someone to blame. The first face he saw was mine.

The other boys backed off, eagerly anticipating a fistfight. I had never been involved in a fight before, but instinctively put my hands up to protect my face. Then a familiar inner voice silently spoke.

"Keep your fists up and dance around," it said. As I began to move around the yard, the voice spoke again: "Jab a little with your right hand." I did this too, even though I was left-handed.

My opponent was looking at me with a little more respect now. I wasn't the 100-percent softy he had supposed. Jabbing the air with my right fist, I made no attempt to hit him. "Hold your big punch until I tell you," said the inner voice. My opponent, forgetting I was left-handed, came at me with fists flailing.

"Now with your left, as hard as you can!" said the voice, and I let fly. My left hook floored the boy; he

15

collapsed like a sack of potatoes. The audience couldn't believe it, and neither could I.

As I stood in line for class, I wondered about the inner voice and the loving clarity of its instructions.

8. The Kiss of God

Lying in bed one evening in March 1968, I was doing my usual review of the day when something quite extraordinary happened. It was so removed from the world of daily experience that I couldn't speak about it for several years afterward. I was twelve years old.

I was suddenly elevated to a plane of being so far beyond my dreams, so far beyond the compass of my mind and imagination, that I was stunned.

An incredible joy gripped me. The love flooding my heart was almost unbearable. The elevation of this wonderful state was immeasurably greater than any I had ever experienced. All doubts and questions, all darkness and confusion, dissolved completely.

It was heaven, full of the Light and Sound of God. This Light and Sound would be the sustenance for my life for several years to come.

Despite the overwhelming sense of fullness, the experience brought with it the simultaneous awareness that there were even higher levels of heaven beyond this one, and yet this hardly seemed possible, so great was my joy.

17

The experience had no association with Jesus, the Catholic church, or any of the Catholic saints. I didn't think of it in religious terms at all. Rather, it was wholly new and original. I had the sense of renewing an old friendship: Associations in my mind pointed to events buried far back in the past, traces of earlier experiences which I couldn't quite recall.

The love was immense; I was soaking in it. Eventually, after perhaps an hour or more, I turned on my side and prepared for sleep. As I lay there with my head on the pillow, I wondered if this heavenly gift would be gone by morning.

But it wasn't gone. As I dressed the next day, I tried to imagine what I must look like. If what I was experiencing within was apparent in any physical sense, I'd have difficulty facing others. What would my family say? Or my friends?

With some reluctance I ventured into the kitchen for breakfast. I half-expected my family to exclaim, "Hey, Robert, what happened to you?" To my relief, no one seemed to notice.

Nor did anyone at school detect a change. My friends were their usual selves. All this time I was so elevated I could hardly contain my joy. There was lightness and excellence everywhere, in everything.

An experience like this is hard to explain. I had no idea what it meant; it was much too personal to discuss with others. In the months that followed I composed dozens of verbal descriptions of the event and recited them to myself, testing their power to evoke some fragmentary memory of the experience, its impact, its heavenly surge of freedom and unearthly stillness.

After many attempts I eventually accepted defeat and settled instead on a simple statement that would act as a marker in later life. It was only a reminder: "When I die I will go to heaven, and that is all that matters." This little phrase was my only article of faith prior to finding ECKANKAR. It was, rather, an article of proven experience. When I came to ECKANKAR, I recognized the experience as the ECKshar, the state of Self-Realization.

Ever so gradually over the ensuing months, the high state faded but didn't entirely disappear. Perhaps I simply adjusted to it. Only later would I lose it.

9. Ubi Quando

The teacher was analyzing some verse by an English poet. While my mind worked on the lesson, I also attended to an unexpected visit from an old friend. Standing quietly in my inner vision, bathed in a nimbus of soft white light, my guardian angel greeted me.

These visits were very special, and I greatly cherished them. His presence was very uplifting. The other boys seemed unaware that anyone was there.

On this occasion he told me his name. Since I had often thought of him simply as my guardian angel, I pondered what he had said in the silent language of the spiritual travelers: "Ubi Quando."

From my Latin classes I knew that *ubi* meant "where." *Quando* meant "when." When previously given other sacred words by my guardian angel, I had recited them to myself throughout the day; they were uplifting in a way I didn't quite understand. I was delighted to know Ubi Quando's name. It brought his presence closer to me.

The significance of *ubi* (where) and *quando* (when) was revealed to me later. Ubi Quando was showing me that heaven is *here* and *now;* the spiritual travelers, the ECK Masters, live and work always in the present moment.

That was 1969. In 1975, when I read my first books on ECKANKAR, I understood. The ECK Master Fubbi Quantz gave me a warm greeting when I made the connection.

10. Peeling Away the Universe

When I was fourteen, I began developing a number of techniques to get to a state of "otherness." It was Soul Travel, though at the time I was unaware of that.

One method I used rested on a very simple premise: As Soul I create all things through my faculty of imagination, and this becomes my reality. So I had only to visualize the reverse process to project myself outside the worlds of creation. It was that simple.

Lying in bed one night, I tried this technique for the first time. Certain of success, I brimmed with enthusiasm. With eyes closed, I gazed softly into that point between the eyebrows, which I was later to learn is called the Spiritual Eye. Next I pictured all that my mind could conceive on one vast canvas. This included all my ideas about man and God.

Then I simply peeled away the corner of the canvas, thereby causing everything to disappear into nothingness. That instant I was catapulted out of my body into a vast empty universe!

The shock was so great that, within a few

seconds, I was pulled straight back into my body again.

The technique had worked. I was delighted! Over the succeeding weeks I refined it further. Yet, whatever improvements I made, I was unable to use it to get to where I really wanted to be—on that level where I had experienced the pure Light and Sound of God two years before.

Chapter Two

Welcome Home

11. Trapdoor

The summer of 1971 was wonderful. The sun shone brilliantly, both within and without, and I enjoyed great vitality and happiness. My inner guardian was at hand whenever I needed reassurance. Experiences with the holy Light and Sound of God were a source of continual upliftment.

My life lacked nothing. Everything went well: studies, sports, relationships, health. It hardly seemed possible to enjoy a greater degree of happiness and inner peace in this world.

Then in mid-September, it all disappeared. It was like falling through a trapdoor. I learned later from my readings that some have called this the dark night of Soul.

Oubliette is a colorful term for a dungeon with neither a door nor windows. The victim is simply dropped down through a hole in the ceiling. The opening is sealed, and the incarcerated victim is simply forgotten (*oublier* in French meaning "to forget"). In the dark night of Soul one feels totally forgotten, as if one has slipped inadvertently from God's sight.

When this first hit me, I was deeply perplexed. Everything changed, almost overnight, but I could find nothing to point to what might have caused this. My emotions were in a turmoil; a storm of confusion tore my inner world asunder. Losing all interest in study, my performance at school dropped alarmingly. Relationships grew tense and difficult.

The world reflected back to me the same images and activities that it did before, but now they seemed unreal, a parody of their former meaning.

During this period my appetite for living drained away. Until then an unquestioned source of life had always nourished my subconscious. But suddenly I could no longer perceive it.

Having taken the Light and Sound for granted since age twelve, I had not known what it would mean to lose them. It was as if a Technicolor movie had suddenly switched to black and white, and the lovely theme music in the background had simply stopped. Everybody on the screen looked and sounded exactly the same, but there was a vast difference.

The hardest part of my dark night of Soul was that I felt acutely alone. I was hardly able to detect the inner presence of my guardian, who had been with me since age two. Had I been thrown into an oubliette, I could not have been more alone and terrified.

My techniques for leaving the body—peeling away the universe, reviewing the day, gazing into my Spiritual Eye, or repeating certain charged words— didn't work during this period. In a sense, the inner worlds were shut off. My dreams brought very limited clarity.

The dark night of Soul is not a psychiatric condition or clinical depression. One can be in the depths of it and have perfect physical, emotional, and mental health. I doubt if more than a few people at that time suspected that inside I dwelt in a living hell.

I never thought seriously about ending my life, although I did wonder at the time why this was so. What kept me going? Being a very tenacious person, I persisted in my search simply because I wanted to know. I discovered that the dark night of Soul is a paradox. Its whole purpose is to sharpen Soul's desire to survive, to stir one consciously to pursue the Light and Sound of God with every ounce of energy and resolve one can muster.

Even now I wonder how I kept my sanity during that period. It lasted exactly four years, from September 1971 to August 1975. From time to time during those four years I caught a glimpse of the Light, like being on a train which suddenly emerges from a tunnel in the mountains for just a brief moment. These tantalizing glimpses kept me going.

I did not know it at the time, but my falling through the trapdoor coincided with the translation (death) of the ECK Master Paul Twitchell, in September 1971. And though it did not seem so at the time, my dark night of Soul would turn out to be a blessing in disguise.

12. Throat Chakra

What is the best approach to truth? Assuming you want it—and I did, to an overwhelming degree—what should you do to obtain it? Faith and belief were all very well, but what should you *do?* For me, this was the crux of the whole matter.

As I saw it, the only way that held promise was to leave my body and see the higher worlds for myself. Anything else seemed futile and secondhand.

One technique for "otherness" which I developed while in this dark night of Soul went roughly as follows: I sat in a semitrance state, which wasn't always easy to induce, and placed my attention on an energy center in my throat. I was not aware at that time that similar techniques had been developed by others. By repeating a word I had received from within, I would leave my body without difficulty and explore a world not unlike earth, but much lighter in atmosphere and vibration. The individuals I met there were very interesting.

These journeys, which usually occurred while traveling home by bus each evening, convinced me that I was on the right track. But, while these out-of-body journeys were refreshing, the technique was limited. I never seemed to be able to get to a higher plane. Why was this?

I learned later that the ECK Masters teach that one should always start by placing the attention at the Spiritual Eye, that point between the eyebrows where Soul resides in the waking state. Soul Travel is often easiest from this area. Lower energy centers, such as the throat chakra, can give only limited results.

After practicing the technique for a few months around the end of 1973, I gave it up. But my experiences set me on a program of intensive reading in psychology and metaphysics which prepared me for finding ECKANKAR.

13. The Holy Sword

While lying on a park bench one day, looking at the sky, I wrestled with the old problems: pain and death, truth and freedom, grace and sin, and so forth. Each chain of thought seemed to collapse in upon itself. The summer of 1974 was dragging its heels and, in the process, grinding me down.

Tiring of the struggle I closed my eyes and watched the branches above my head scatter soft shadows across my eyelids. I had been lying there for about fifteen minutes when, without warning, a blade of white light cut down through my head like a sword.

In that instant, all of my confusion completely— if momentarily—dissolved. I saw everything with total clarity.

The illumination lasted no more than a few seconds. Shaken but elated, I jumped up and hastened home to record these precious pearls of wisdom before they faded from memory. As I dashed back to the house, I tried as swiftly as I could to piece together the fragments of the experience as they filtered through my mind.

But I just couldn't do it. The instant on the park bench could not be dissected into concepts, labels, and rules.

I realized that if I needed truth that badly I would have to allow the same experience to recur, on a regular basis if necessary.

But how?

14. Vairag—Detached Love

From time to time I came across a shred of information which seemed strangely relevant to my quest. One spring I began a microscopic study of the New Testament, hoping to hit upon some clues which would help satisfy my terrible hunger for truth.

I also searched many volumes of religious, philosophical, and metaphysical subjects. Extra attendance at church, to squeeze the last drop of comfort from a distant deity, left me drained, more lonely than ever.

Short passages in books stood out occasionally, quietly suggesting a new direction in my quest. The works of the Trappist monk Thomas Merton were very rewarding in this respect.

In one book he asked if there were twenty men alive in the world today who could see truth in all its simplicity, who were completely free of the influence of any created thing or heavenly gift, even the most supernaturally pure of God's graces.

He didn't believe there were twenty but concluded that "there must be one or two. They are the ones who are holding everything together and keeping the universe from falling apart."

This thought burned into my heart. Who were these guys? I needed to know.

15. Dream Direction

On December 17, 1973, I made my way to work as usual. All day I could think about only one thing, a message I had received in my dreams the previous night. It was simple: to give up work and attend college the following year.

In the dream my guardian angel had finally reappeared. He'd given the instruction, stating that I'd meet someone at the university who would give me some information of vital importance in my search for truth.

My heart and head were in a turmoil. Why was I being asked to give up my job? Had I not made enough sacrifices in my search for truth? Although nothing within me or in the outer world was making much sense these days, I still wondered why I was being asked to bring more disruption to my life.

The reason became apparent in April 1975. Enrolled in the local university, I was standing in the school cafeteria, downstairs by the north window. The girl I was with had just received two books on loan from a friend. They were called *In My Soul I Am Free* and *Letters to Gail,* Volume I. She excitedly began telling me about them.

When she spoke the words *Paul Twitchell* and *ECKANKAR,* I received quite a shock. I felt as if she had just tapped me softly on the back of the head with a wooden mallet. Little did I know what this would mean to my future and how these books would be the instrument to propel me out of my dark night of Soul.

16. An Old Friend

Around this time, I had another rather curious experience. On a day when I had sunk to one of my lowest points, something I would later know as the ECK, the Holy Spirit, stepped in unexpectedly to give me assistance.

I was gazing into a bookstore window during my lunch break when I noticed an old lady clad entirely in black. She was standing behind me. Without an introduction, she began speaking to my reflection in the window as though we were already well acquainted.

Turning around, I acknowledged her with a bemused smile. She continued talking in a warm, encouraging tone, her lively statements peppered with laughter and chuckles. Her manner and presence were most unusual, and I listened intently to what she said.

Speaking about poets and playwrights, she touched upon some cardinal spiritual themes: be determined to reach your goal, hang in there, ignore ridicule, drop your sense of grievance and resentment.

Her simple stories conveyed clear messages as she waved her cloth shopping bag to emphasize a point. Every now and then she took on a distant look and repeated a particular phrase for my benefit, as though she were quoting an ancient source. She clearly wanted me to remember it.

Then she stopped quite suddenly, bade me good-bye, and walked away. As she left she said, "We'll meet again soon."

My encounter with this strange old woman and her sparkling words greatly uplifted me that day. I learned later that the ECK Masters may make brief appearances amid the seeming chaos and jumble of our worldly existence, to bring us help in our mundane affairs. This may happen only a few times in our lives. It usually comes at a critical juncture, when we feel most alone, most in need of reassurance and support.

17. Magician or Master?

My friend at university had offered to loan me one of the books on ECKANKAR. But I refused at the time. Given the effect Paul Twitchell's name had on me, I immediately assumed he was a white magician. I had been having a lot of trouble with psychic attacks and interference during those years, so I kept well clear of anyone who mixed the psychic with the spiritual.

About a week later I relented. I asked for *Letters to Gail* on loan, and over the weekend read it cover to cover, hardly believing anyone could treat the topic of spirituality so expertly, with an authority born of experimentation and experience.

Over the following months, still trying to decide if Paul Twitchell was magician or Master, I read several of the authors he highly recommended: Saint John of the Cross, Thomas Merton, and Saint Teresa of Avila. I also had a strong attraction to Psalms, which Paul recommended. This was a very painful period for me. I somehow knew that everything hinged on how I solved the riddle of Paul Twitchell.

The crisis came to a head in July. I was working in a canning factory. The sense of total alienation of the dark night of Soul was almost crushing me. So, as I worked, I began repeating to myself the most charged words I knew, which happened to be the titles of the four ECKANKAR books I had just ordered via mail.

"The Tiger's Fang, In My Soul I Am Free, The Flute of God, The Far Country," I chanted under my breath. The seemingly innocent words became a mantra, a connecting link with the spiritual presence I missed so much.

And suddenly the weight began to lift.

On the strength of that one book, *Letters to Gail,* and the experience I had in July, I ordered a dozen ECKANKAR books and signed up as a member of ECKANKAR in August. The first time I tried the Spiritual Exercises of ECK, sitting alone on the floor next to my bed, the room filled with a soft, pale blue light.

After four years in darkness, this was an immense joy and relief. My heart soared, and my dark night of Soul came to an end.

18. The Sun

During the same week, I received another dream message from Fubbi Quantz. In it the ECK Master directed me to buy oil-painting supplies and try reproducing an image that was continually appearing in my inner vision.

The image had been haunting me for weeks, slipping into my thoughts in so tantalizing a way that I felt compelled to capture it on canvas.

The finished work brought a lovely wave of relief. I contemplated the painting for days; it was deeply satisfying in a way I had never expected.

On August 26, 1975, I got a heartwarming surprise when I opened the package of ECKANKAR books I had ordered from the United States. The cover of the ECK book *In My Soul I Am Free* carried the same image I had painted—a glowing orange sun exploding into white.

This was one of the many special ways that I heard, "Welcome home."

Chapter Three

Soul Travel

19. Garden

In my early years as a member of ECKANKAR, I attempted to learn controlled Soul Travel. I would sit still and focus my attention on the Sound and Light of God. The Sound usually carried me beyond the physical state of awareness.

To accomplish this, I would gently hold in my Spiritual Eye the image of an enclosed garden. If I did this long enough I would gradually identify with that state. Without seeing, I would see the flowers and shrubs, the manicured lawn, the shimmering pool with its small cascading fountain, and the mossy archway at the entrance.

This was my garden, a quiet place where I alone could enter and rest undisturbed. Sitting on an old wooden bench, I would shuffle the gravel beneath my feet and listen to the rippling waters of the fountain or sweet birdsong from the branches overhead.

There were two side gates, both locked. Since this was my special place, no one else had access. I was only getting used to controlled Soul Travel at that time and still had a lot of difficulty with the mind's interference, so I found it very comforting to have this security, to rest in a familiar place.

I was studying now with the Mahanta, the Living ECK Master. As my inner guide, he often got me to visit places which evoked strong sensory images—the crunch of snow under my feet, the hiss of waves receding on a sandy beach, the cry of gulls overhead. These helped develop my faculty for remembering what took place in my inner travels. It built my confidence in those early days.

I realized that the big question for me was not, *How do I learn Soul Travel?* but *How do I become more conscious that I am already Soul traveling?*

This was my challenge.

20. The Swing

Though I was having a number of subtle Soul Travel experiences during my first years in ECKANKAR, I was very reluctant to accept their reality.

In a spiritual exercise during that time, I saw a house set among rambling green meadows on a great estate. To the left lay an enclosed ornamental garden where the Mahanta stood, awaiting my arrival. By his side stood a Higher Initiate, a member of the ECKANKAR clergy, whom I recognized.

When she saw me arrive in my cautious, unsure way — so typical at that time — she laughed and said, "He still thinks he is imagining things!"

The Mahanta took hold of my hands and swung me around and around to demonstrate, more surely than words, the reality of my experience.

This amusing Soul Travel experience helped cure me of my timidity.

21. Concerto

Not long after becoming a member of ECKANKAR, I awoke one morning with a beautiful piece of music floating in my consciousness. The Mahanta had taken me in a dream to a concert on the inner planes.

We sat in a very large auditorium listening to the best orchestra I had ever heard. The final piece lasted about fifteen minutes or so, and I awoke just as it ended.

For days this lovely music drifted in and out of my mind, leaving a delicious impression. But I couldn't identify the piece.

About twelve months later I was listening to a live concert broadcast on national radio. Since I had tuned in after the program had started, I didn't hear the announcer introduce the first piece. To my surprise, it was the same work I had heard in the dream state the previous year.

Sitting quiet as a mouse, I listened for the announcement. Which musical work had the Mahanta taken me to hear in the dream state? It was one of Prokofiev's concertos. For me the music from my dream had always been an allegory of Soul's upward journey.

This experience gave me a better understanding of the way Soul Travel works and how the Holy Spirit, the ECK, strikes a balance between inner and outer activities.

22. Visit to Agam Des

The truths of heaven are written in a series of spiritual texts called the Shariyat-Ki-Sugmad, found in the various planes of God, including this earth plane. As I was unfolding spiritually, I had an experience with the Shariyat which showed me its potential beyond an external expression in book form.

Around my two-year mark in ECKANKAR, just before my Second Initiation, the ECK Master Fubbi Quantz appeared in my inner vision just as I was about to drop off to sleep. A beautiful sapphire glow radiated from him, and his eyes were like two stars.

With little ceremony, he ushered me in the Soul body to the spiritual city of Agam Des. This unfolded so quickly that I could scarcely comprehend what was happening.

We arrived at a huge vaulted temple which shone brightly with creamy hues. Fubbi was very composed. As he pointed toward a lean figure walking toward us, my eyes opened wide. This was the first time I had encountered Yaubl Sacabi, the fabled ECK Master and guardian of the second section of the Shariyat at the city of Agam Des. Yaubl greeted me quietly.

The ECK Masters were probably being a little

less vocal than usual to enable me to contain my excitement. The guardian of the Shariyat let me take a look around before leading me down a stairway to our right. Fubbi followed.

The stairway was steep and seemed to alternate between extremes of brightness and darkness as we descended. After we had gone some distance, another chamber opened before us, though not nearly so large as the first. The walls about us radiated a warm greenish glow.

Yaubl pointed to a small altar. Resting on top was the Shariyat. Following carefully behind the Master, I reached out and gently touched the open text. The volume was thousands of pages thick and bound in brownish leather. The text was small and neat, crammed with divine knowledge and written in a script which I had never seen before.

The feeling came to me to push the pages lightly with my right hand. As I did so, they began to leaf across without actually moving.

The whole experience touched me deeply. Turning to Yaubl, I exclaimed, "The pages seem to be without number!"

"Who can measure the wisdom of SUGMAD?" he replied, laughing.

Letting the pages settle where they would, I read the first paragraph that met my eyes, about eight lines. But I was unable to recall them later. The meaning seemed unusually apt. Then the guardian indicated that it was time to leave.

While Fubbi brought me upstairs again, Yaubl closed the gate to the inner sanctum. With that, I found myself back in bed.

23. Shamus-i-Tabriz

Exactly a week after the journey to Agam Des, another very vivid Soul Travel adventure left a deep mark on my consciousness.

Just as I was about to drop off to sleep, I found myself walking through a tranquil forest, drinking in the splendor and beauty of the scene. After a while I came to the edge of the forest where, in place of the earth, a huge bank of rolling white clouds stretched before me. The forest, it seemed, was an island in the sky.

In the distance, perched high in the luminescent whiteness, was a medieval castle. As I stood there, gazing across at the marvelous structure and wishing I could be there, a narrow carpet unrolled slowly from the castle's gate to my feet.

The moment I stepped onto the carpet, the Mahanta appeared. Without a word, he signaled for me to follow.

When at length we reached the castle, I discovered its great gate was really a dense curtain of dark blue mist, a velvety softness very pleasing to behold. Hesitating a little, I entered, trusting the Mahanta to guide me safely through. We stepped into a scene of such light and splendor that it outshone anything I had seen thus far. In my mind I was comparing it with the light of Agam Des.

The Mahanta led me down a narrow side street, a place I would never have thought to go. The buildings on either side seemed to lean forward, casting giant shadows. We arrived eventually at a secluded grotto where the ECK Master Shamus-i-Tabriz was seated.

His imposing presence was a bit unsettling at first. Unlike the ECK Masters I had met up to that time, he was serious and muscular, rocklike and grave. His robe, a deep blue, had the same hue as the velvet gate at the entrance to this great castle in the sky.

As we approached, his appearance softened. Then he spoke. His words came forth slowly. Feeling naked and puny, I stood quietly before him, in awe of this extraordinary man.

His discourse was difficult to grasp. Being a novice at Soul Travel, I had little faculty at that time for recalling the words of the ECK Masters when spoken on the inner planes. With a gesture that bespoke colossal power, he pulled back an immense screen that filled the sky. Brahm, the lord of the lower worlds, began speaking from a vault of darkness.

His discourse was very similar to the one the ECK Master Shamus-i-Tabriz had just given. I stood transfixed.

Then Shamus lowered the screen, covering the voice and the darkness. In a very serious tone, resonating with an awesome mixture of love and power, he slowly uttered the following statement:

"When you can truly distinguish between the meaning of both discourses, you will be fit to travel higher."

This shook me to my roots, and I immediately found myself back home in bed.

24. Woolen Suit

Being low on cash, I couldn't afford a new suit that winter, although I badly needed one. My old sport jacket was looking threadbare, but I reasoned it would last another few months.

That winter I moved into a room in a hostel with two other men; each of us was allocated an empty locker for our clothes. When I went to hang up my clothes, I found a three-piece woolen suit.

What a stroke of good fortune! I thought. I tried the suit on; it fit perfectly. This was doubly fortunate, since few ready-made garments ever fit me correctly without alterations.

But, I reasoned, it probably belonged to someone. I couldn't take it. So I replaced the suit in the room's spare closet and forgot about it until the next morning.

I returned to my room after breakfast, only to discover the suit was lying across my bed. Who had put it there? I wondered. Maybe this was a sign that I should accept it. Still, I had some doubts, so I put it back into the closet.

A few days later the same thing happened: the suit was lying across my bed when I returned to the room one afternoon. Perhaps the cleaning person had put it there. But why put it on my bed? Why move the suit at all?

At this point, I decided to accept the gift.

The former owner never did return for the suit. I realized that if I did the very best I could in each situation, then Divine Spirit would take care of the rest.

25. Silver Coin

In March 1978 I recorded the following dream experience which came at a low point in my life. The dream was very vivid. It affected me for days afterward.

In the dream I was with several other ECKists, gathered around a piano. Paul Twitchell was playing the piano in a lighthearted manner, not at all what I was expecting from a God-Realized individual. I remarked to myself at the time how childlike he was. With a big grin on his face, he played a well-known tune, fingering each note very distinctly.

Then he stopped playing and gave each person a hollow plastic stick, just like a drinking straw. I knew instinctively that, when opened, each stick would reveal something of our spiritual strength.

Paul opened a few for us in a humorous way. He smiled and joked when mine revealed a bright silver coin inside.

This simple experience gave me a great deal of encouragement. The silver coin was a token to admit Soul into the higher planes of heaven. It was an opportunity: How I "spent" it was up to me.

26. Etruscan Museum

About noon on August 19, 1980, I was standing on a stairway in the Etruscan Museum near the Villa Borghese Gardens in Rome. While looking at some artifacts from this ancient civilization, particularly some shields hanging on an opposite wall, I became aware of something peculiar.

A spark of consciousness was in front of me, staring intently at me, hovering between the wall and the staircase. While it was benign, I could tell it was not the presence of an ECK Master.

The vibration radiating from this Soul was excitement, as though It was trying to attract my attention. After about ten seconds or so, It disappeared.

Off and on for the rest of the day I wondered who that Soul could have been. The answer came almost two years later.

On May 15, 1982, I attended an ECKANKAR seminar in Chelsea, London. A young woman came up to me and quietly confided that she had seen me during a spiritual exercise and had tried to communicate with me.

"This was about two years ago, maybe less," she added. "The building looked like a museum or something, and you were standing on a platform."

When one is blessed with vivid experiences in the Soul body, the shortcomings of both the psychic and the cosmic consciousness states become very apparent. The degree of freedom to be found in the Soul body is sharp, sweet, and unconditional. There can be no mistaking the experience.

27. Train Crash

As I was going out the door one morning, I got a brief instruction from the Mahanta: "Bring along a fresh handkerchief." This was a little odd, since I didn't need one. But I took a freshly laundered hankie from the top drawer and stuffed it into my coat pocket.

Taking my usual train to work, I settled down to read the morning paper. En route, the train stalled near a tunnel. This happened every now and then, but that morning the delay was much longer. But I was busy with my paper, and I didn't give the matter a second thought.

Suddenly a massive jolt threw me out of my seat. There was a terrific crashing sound as the train car was lifted into the air. Children screamed as steam rapidly filled the compartment.

I learned later that, due to a signaling fault, another train had struck us from behind.

Only after crawling through the window did I see the full extent of the damage. Several cars had been torn apart or raised several feet off the tracks. Passengers milled around, trying to calm the stricken children, who fortunately weren't badly hurt.

As I made my way up the tracks toward the station I met a neatly dressed gentleman who asked if I was OK. "I'm fine, thanks," I told him. He was about to move along when I called him back. "Did you know you have a bad gash on your forehead?" I asked him, realizing that in all the commotion he probably hadn't noticed his own injury.

What could I do for him? I thought. At that moment the Mahanta whispered, "Robert, give him the hankie."

28. Somebody Special

Two years after I had become a member of ECKANKAR, the Mahanta told me we were going to visit "somebody special." When I saw Lai Tsi, the diminutive Chinese ECK Master, tears came to my eyes.

We embraced. The Chinese Adept gestured to a pair of floor cushions. We sat on the cushions. "What have you been doing all this time, ever since you were my student?"

"But you already know, Master."

"Ah, yes, but do *you* know?"

In a sense this was painful for me. Three thousand years seems such a long time in earth terms, but to Soul it is only a few steps on the journey home to God, the glorious SUGMAD. Having advanced far on my path with Lai Tsi in that lifetime, I made a dreadful blunder. My ego knew no bounds; pride and arrogance were my downfall. As can so easily happen if we are not careful, I followed the dictates of power, not love. I lost all of my initiations and amassed a huge debt to life.

The immediately succeeding lifetimes were

sorrowful in the extreme. The loneliness and pain were almost unbearable as I faced the mountain of karma created by my rebellious attitude. Without the support and comfort of divine love, I had to confront my poisonous reserve of bitterness and anger, tortured by the certain knowledge that I had lost a truly precious opportunity under Lai Tsi, the Mahanta in that cycle of time.

The ECK Master lit up past images in my memory, revealing a succession of lifetimes in various parts of Asia. Then came Egypt, Greece, Rome, and the Middle East. After that came a series of incarnations among the North and Central American Indians. Finally, a sojourn of lifetimes around Europe, the U.S., and Canada. Some of these brought me temporarily into contact again with the Light Giver.

These recollected images could have been very disturbing, but Lai Tsi was careful not to reveal too much. In this way I got a broad overview, a clear insight without the necessity of reexperiencing old and painful emotions.

"Your great problem still is impatience," Lai Tsi said. "Even with me you were impetuous and restless. Now I will tell you a great secret: Suffering can open the heart to love."

Certain past lives had seemed futile, their sufferings for naught. But Lai Tsi was showing me their value, the intimate way they had brought about my deep hunger for God. In that sense, suffering *had* opened my heart to love. Perhaps he was also pointing to the future.

"The ECK will make demands which will cause much inner turmoil and confusion," he added. "The way to overcome all of this, as well as the sharp karmic blows, is via the correct attitude. This attitude can only exist through complete surrender to the Mahanta. Hide not a single iota of your life as 'mine' but open all to the Mahanta, even your doubts about the ancient one. In this way you can ride any storm."

With a gesture of warmth and encouragement, the Master continued: "You will receive a boost of the ECK Current during the spiritual exercise which led to this experience."

Knowing our special meeting was coming to an end, I asked Lai Tsi why the place where we sat was so dark and empty.

"We are in a remote part of the Etheric Plane," he replied. "It is not necessary as yet that you be distracted by the immensity of this world. It is the discourse that counts."

And with that, the experience came to an end.

Chapter Four

We Two

29. The Child Technique

During my first years in ECKANKAR, I experimented with several different Soul Travel techniques. One would work for a while and then fizzle out. So I'd try another. Then it too ceased to work for me.

After a while, I caught on: It seemed my mind was devising clever ways to drown out each technique in turn.

Then I went through a dry period where nothing worked. Nothing was happening in the accepted visual sense, but I realized my life was changing. Yet I wanted clear Soul Travel experiences. My mind was simply getting out of hand. Mulling it over, I got to thinking and came up with an effective technique which has never yet let me down.

I would imagine I was waiting for the Master to come and take me on a short Soul Travel journey. I softly sang HU (pronounced like the word *hue*), the universal name of God. Then I let my image of myself drift back in time to when I was a little child.

Three or so was a good age, I found. I was warm and inquisitive then, full of Soul's zest for new experiences. Most important of all, my ego hadn't yet developed. Thus my mind was less able to block out spontaneous shifts in consciousness.

In this state, where I'd enjoy the feelings and outlook of a child, the Mahanta would come and take me by the hand. Since I was so tiny, he seemed a very tall individual indeed. With loving trust, I'd toddle off by his side.

I used this technique on a purely imaginary level the first few times I practiced it. Soon I noticed something else occurring, something subtle but distinct.

To use this technique effectively, I found it was very important to be kind and forgiving with myself, accepting with childlike gratitude the Mahanta's helping hand.

30. Of Car Trouble and Granola

Emily and I were members of a hill-walking club. I had known her for about a year before I actually began to notice her. I found out later that this was because until the end of 1980 she smoked. The smoke clouded her aura to the point where I couldn't see her as the beautiful Soul she is.

We began dating in February 1981 and got engaged in April of the same year. Once I'd recognized Emily, marriage was the natural step. We had been together before, so our marriage was really a continuation of many old relationships from past incarnations.

We talked a lot about ECKANKAR in those months before we married, and we were both going through some inner cleansing. Some of hers manifested as car trouble.

During one particular period Emily wanted to rush some things in her life but go slowly with others. This attitude was governed by a lot of mentalizing rather than a true inner feeling of what the right pace should be. Not long after that the timing chain, the device on her car which regulates the rhythm of the engine, snapped. Other incidents resulted in numerous scratches and dents.

I was also going through some cleansing prior to our marriage. I realized my current health problems could be helped by a regular diet of a chewy cereal called granola.

I bought the ingredients and made up a batch. Unfortunately the mixture required so much chewing that I spent ages at breakfast each morning, sometimes running late for work. This couldn't go on, I thought. I couldn't give over half my life to munching like a sheep.

I asked for help during contemplation and was shown an image of an electric blender. The message was clear: Use the blender to grind the granola into a finer consistency that would be easier to chew. I wondered where to get such a machine.

The next day I happened to be talking to my mother on the phone and mentioned my experience. Laughing, she told me that one of my cousins had just dropped off a wedding present: an electric blender.

31. Wedding Suit

With my wedding coming up in a week, I needed a new suit. I often had trouble finding ready-to-wear clothing that would fit me without extensive alterations. To avoid the unpleasant task of trekking from store to store to find something that would fit my slight build, I asked the Mahanta to show me what was needed.

During contemplation that evening I saw an image of the perfect suit: it was lovely, and it fit me! The next morning, full of expectations, I set off to the city to shop.

The first store I tried was Anderson's. Surprisingly I found the exact suit I had seen in contemplation the previous evening. This is too easy, I thought. Perhaps there was something even better around the next corner. Perhaps the ECK had something really spectacular lined up for me if only I persisted. So I continued to look.

The wedding suit trek took me across the city, from store to store, examining hundreds of garments and trying on over a dozen. Worn out and a little dejected, I decided to try Bellingham's, the most expensive store in town. They were bound to have what I wanted.

After putting up with my fussy ways for about half an hour, the tall sales assistant looked snootily down at me and in a droll voice intoned, "Perhaps you would like to try the boys' department at Anderson's?"

Annoyed at the salesman's put-down, I headed back to Anderson's. There I discovered that the perfect suit, the one I had tried on first that morning, was actually in the boys' department.

Tired and wiser, I bought it. Sometimes the guidance of the ECK can be so direct that we ignore it, thinking the correct course surely must be more complicated.

32. Tip-off

Emily and I wanted to build a new home and finally found a lot that we both liked very much. We hired a construction company and were required to pay 10 percent of the final price in advance, as a deposit. The last payment would be due in eight weeks.

That week in contemplation I was given a tip-off that shook me: the ECK-Vidya, the ancient science of prophecy, opened up and showed me the construction company going bust very soon. I told Emily about this. What if we lost our deposit before the close of the sale?

It was a difficult time period for us, but we made it to the closing without the company going bust. As we walked out of the office with our closing papers signed and intact, I wondered if my prophetic experience had been true after all.

Shortly after the close of the sale, the construction company collapsed. Because it was the biggest in the state, the businesses in the area were in shock. No one had predicted this.

The ECK-Vidya, the ancient science of prophecy,

sometimes gives a person an unsolicited look at the future for his own protection. The most difficult part of this science is determining the precise time a future event is scheduled to occur.

33. Sowing the Seed

When we moved into our new home, the back-yard was just a plot of untilled topsoil. I braced myself for the task ahead—preparing the ground for planting. I dug for several weeks, becoming stiff and sore. With this task completed, I let the soil lie fallow for a few months so that any weed seedlings could mature and be removed easily by hand.

My plan was to sow grass seed over the plot in the fall. The warmth of summer would still linger in the soil, I reasoned, which would allow the seeds to germinate and grow a little before winter. By spring the lawn would be partially established and have a head start on any invading weeds.

But the time left for sowing grass seed before winter was fast running out. The weather had been very damp. So I made a thought mold for good weather. Would I be fortunate enough to have a dry weekend? I wondered.

The next morning was warm and radiant with sunshine. The soil dried quickly in the cloudless calm. It took only a few hours to get the grass seed scattered evenly over the topsoil and gently rake it into the ground.

But the dry weather continued. Now there was no rain to germinate the seeds! The soil got harder with each passing day, so rather than wait for a change, I made another strong thought mold, this time for rain.

And it soon came, in bucketfulls. It rained night and day. It wouldn't stop! Weeks passed without a dry spell. The yard was eventually flooded, and all the seed I had so carefully sown got washed away.

When it finally did germinate, we had a thick green fringe around the edge of the yard—the center was completely bare.

The spiritual laws cannot be bent to suit our purpose. We must instead become attuned to the workings of the Holy Spirit. Then we can enter into a reciprocal relationship based on love and trust, allowing this divine force of God to handle our affairs in the best way for our unfoldment.

The use of thought power has no place in the spiritual life.

34. The Mahanta Loves You

One day soon after we moved, my wife and I took a walk with some friends. Our route meandered through a large meadow about a mile from our home.

Wandering some distance ahead of the group I spied two elderly ladies and a dog approaching from the edge of the field. Following an inner nudge, I called the dog over. She was shy at first and seemed reluctant to approach, but with warm words I encouraged her to come nearer.

"The Mahanta loves you, little one," I said. This seemed like a strange thing to say, and I wondered why I felt like passing on the message. But at my words she came right over and allowed me to pet her.

I kept repeating the phrase, and the dog became ecstatic, lying down and letting me stroke her tummy. I could feel her soaking up the love, drinking it in with her full attention.

By this time my friends and the two ladies had arrived. The older lady looked down at the dog with an awed expression and exclaimed, "That's amazing! I don't believe it!"

Her friend was mute with surprise. The woman continued, "The dog never lets anybody touch her!"

The woman explained that when the dog was a pup, her owner had mistreated her brutally, inflicting emotional scars which had left her in terror of humans, especially men. Under no circumstances would the dog let anyone touch her, except the woman who was her present owner.

We said good-bye to the two ladies, and I stroked the dog once more, then continued on our way. The little miracle stayed in my mind as an example of the Mahanta's love for all Souls and how it could touch even the most hidden heart.

35. The Big Bang

The night was clear and fresh. As we drove home, my wife and I discussed our plans for the future. On a long, empty stretch of road, a car slowly emerged from a concealed entrance. An oncoming car, traveling at high speed, swerved to avoid the first car and pulled right across the divider into our lane. We were on a collision course.

What could we do? There was no room to swerve to avoid the car. At the same time, it hardly seemed possible that this was happening. Without thinking, I immediately tensed my body for the certain impact.

As I did so, an inner voice spoke softly. "Relax. Sit back, Robert. You'll be all right."

And I did. After smashing into the oncoming car, we hit a lamppost.

Apart from a temporary loss of breath as the seatbelt tightened on impact, I was OK. My wife, who was driving, had a distinct mark on her forehead where she had struck the steering wheel. But other than that we were both unhurt.

The Mahanta had taken care of us; the car,

however, was a mess. The front end and engine were crushed, the chassis twisted, and the right front wheel ripped off.

The driver of the other car was also miraculously unhurt.

Even though we both felt fine, the police insisted we get a proper medical exam. Some friends who happened to arrive on the scene at that moment took us to the hospital. The examining doctor had dealt with many motorists injured on that stretch of road. It greatly surprised him that we were showing none of the usual signs of stress or shock.

I was still unsure of the purpose of the accident. Had I said or done something that necessitated it? Was there some old karmic debt needing to be paid?

It wasn't until the next day that I remembered a request I had made to the Mahanta the evening before the accident. My outer and inner life recently had been rather uneventful, so I had asked for a really special experience, something that would pack a wallop.

I chuckled to myself when I put two and two together. And I resolved always to let the Mahanta determine the pace of my unfoldment and the experiences I needed.

36. Fast Track

Our car was written off as a total loss due to the collision. We rented a car until we could purchase a new one. My wife said that the rental car would probably be covered by our insurance. Having almost been killed by an irresponsible motorist, it was the least they could do to provide us with good transportation.

I wasn't so sure. I felt so fortunate to be in one piece that I wanted to go light on the rental, even if we had to do without transportation for a few weeks. A car crash is a big bundle of karma, I argued. I wanted to get off as lightly as possible.

I was mulling over our disagreement one afternoon while I walked down a busy city street. Both points of view seemed valid, yet we had to soon adopt one of them to make a decision on whether or not to keep the rental car.

Inwardly I asked the Mahanta for help. I needed to know the correct solution—and get some kind of verification of the best course of action.

As I approached a pedestrian crossing, I noticed a handsome new green sports car parked in the walkway. A lady in the passenger seat evidently thought this was a good opportunity to alight and opened the door. A cyclist speeding past didn't have a chance. He went splat against the door and fell in a heap at my feet.

Everybody froze. The lady was glued to her seat; the driver of the sports car didn't budge. The other pedestrians took a moment to adjust to the suddenness of this dramatic event. Meanwhile, the lone cyclist was picking himself up off the ground.

I felt that this out-of-the-ordinary event might be the ECK's way of giving me an answer to the rental car question. I decided that if the bicyclist sped off with just a few angry words, I was right. If the sports-car owner had to make retribution, then my wife was right and we would keep the rental car.

The cyclist awkwardly pulled himself together and glared menacingly at the petrified woman. Then he slowly bent down and picked up his shiny tenspeed racing bike. Looking at him, I knew that if the bicycle was damaged there was going to be war. Both wheels turned. Nothing was buckled.

The rider looked as though he was about to mount his bicycle but paused a moment to adjust his ruffled clothing. This meant he had to lean the bicycle against something. With a sharp, satisfied motion, he slammed it against the front fender of the car, scratching it a little. The driver was clearly horrified but felt so paralyzed by circumstances that he remained in his seat.

Having straightened his garments, the cyclist then calmly mounted his bicycle and sped off.

I felt that the answer was clear. I phoned my wife

that afternoon and agreed to keep the rental car for a few more weeks. As matters turned out, the insurance company didn't dispute the additional expense.

Chapter Five

Beautiful Dreamer

37. Three Questions

I was applying for a promotion to a new job within my company, and the interview had been scheduled for that afternoon. With about an hour to go, I was trying to relax at my desk.

My boss was in good spirits and began telling me stories about his own promotion interviews. To help get me warmed up, he asked me three questions. They were a bit off the beaten track, and I handled them poorly.

Seeing my knowledge was deficient in this area, my boss kindly spelled out the textbook answers to the three questions. Then I set off for the interview.

Everything went very well. The board members asked all the right questions—the ones I could answer easily. With only five minutes left, I knew I'd get through if I wasn't tripped in the closing moments.

One interviewer, sitting to my left, had been silent until now. During the pause, he cleared his throat, looked me in the eye, and fired three questions at me.

They were identical to the three my boss had asked and answered for me earlier in the day.

With such good preparation, courtesy of the Mahanta, I got the job.

38. Translation

When my friend's mother passed on, it was a complete surprise to everybody. A very oppressive atmosphere hung over the house as everyone tried to accept her translation.

Some months later, at about 11:00 p.m. the deceased woman called out my friend's name in a loud and troubled voice. From their respective bedrooms the other members of the household also heard her call. By her plaintive tone they knew she was asking for help.

My friend came to visit me the following day. He knew a little about ECKANKAR from our conversations, although he was not a member himself. He asked if there was anything I could do to help. He thought the Mahanta might be able to help resolve this unusual spiritual conflict.

That night during contemplation, I felt the considerable psychic discomfort the woman was experiencing. I softly sang HU and asked the Mahanta if he could work with this troubled Soul. Perhaps he could ease her tight grip on this universe.

After I had made this request, I fell asleep and thought no more about it.

A few days passed, and I called my friend. He related the beneficial change that had occurred in the household. The heavy tension had lifted, and the woman had made no further attempts to contact the family. She had apparently settled down in her new home.

39. Satori

In my studies of ECKANKAR, I have learned that all paths and religions are recognized by the ECK Masters as valid in their own right. In order to learn more about the different spiritual training grounds that exist for Soul on the way to meet the Mahanta, I was reading a book on Zen Buddhism.

Zen seemed a good teaching for people given to intense mental activity. According to the Zen teachings, the goal was satori, the moment of sudden illumination when Soul perceives reality directly without the confusing intrusion of the mind.

Pondering this, I set out for the office.

While doing some morning chores at work, I was sipping a cup of tea and reflecting on the laws of Spirit as expressed in Zen Buddhism. What were the ECK Masters doing which was so far beyond mind and no-mind? Maybe this could only be known through personal experience. These questions rippled back and forth in my thoughts. Knowing how the ECK works, I figured I'd get an answer someday.

Around midmorning I went to the washroom to

clean my cup. Being near the center of the building, the room had no windows. The walls and the floor were covered with hard ceramic tiles. As I stood by the paper-towel dispenser slowly drying my cup, my mind went back to Zen.

"Mahanta, what is satori?" I asked.

That instant there was an explosion. My consciousness leaped in tune with the shock of sound.

Looking down, I saw my cup on the tile floor. It must have slipped from the towel and shattered on impact. In that small enclosed space the sound was greatly magnified. Laughing, I bent down and gathered up the fragments.

The Mahanta had certainly answered my question. The ECK can sometimes give Soul a short, sharp shock to wrench It free of an old state of consciousness and establish a whole new mode of perception.

There was more to this experience. I felt I should bring home the fragments and try to reconstruct the cup. That evening, using some glue, I completed the task. When I went to fill the cup I saw that there was a tiny hole in the side. I was certain I had picked up all the pieces, even down to the tiniest fragment. Yet with nothing left out, a tiny space still remained.

The Mahanta resolved the question for me later in contemplation: That's the tiny hole through which Soul escapes the mind.

40. Beautiful Dreamer

Having joined a music library, I was eager to try out some new material. I borrowed several works by my favorite composers, then decided to experiment with a little twentieth-century music. So I took home a piece by Boulez and two by Berg.

All three were difficult works, very much in the modern vein. After listening to the Boulez piece twice, I sat through both of the Berg compositions. Though they were intellectually interesting, they did nothing to uplift me. If anything, their lack of love and harmony was somewhat disturbing.

The experiment over, I put the records away.

The next day I felt dreadful. There was nothing the matter with me physically, but the usual steady hum of energy was gone. For some reason I felt very disoriented. As the hours passed there came no sign that this fog might lift. I felt as though I had been taken apart and reassembled in the wrong order.

Toward evening I became more concerned. My wife was as puzzled by the whole thing as I was. So before going to sleep that night I asked the Mahanta for an understanding of what was happening and how I might heal it.

In a dream I visited the home of an ECK High Initiate. She greeted me, and I asked her if I could use her phone book to find the number of the electric company. I searched the whole book but couldn't find it. Yet when I handed the book to her, she found the number almost immediately.

The following morning I recorded the dream in my journal. The act of writing down the details brought through the dream's full meaning. My energy centers were being interfered with. The High Initiate had been working on a painting at the time of my visit; I took this as a sign that the art I had been absorbing into my personal atmosphere was the cause of all my difficulties.

The message was clear. The music had poisoned me!

The disruptive vibrations had seriously upset my emotional, or Astral, body. If I was to undo the damage without having to work through more pain and upset as my inner bodies adjusted, I'd need a suitable piece of warmhearted, melodic music to restore my natural harmony.

As I went downstairs for breakfast, I thanked the Mahanta for kindly revealing the cause of my predicament. Walking into the kitchen, I heard a bright, fresh tune emanating from the radio: "Beautiful Dreamer" by Steven Foster.

"That's for you," the Inner Master said with a smile.

This lovely song was the answer. I hummed it the whole day, while shaving, walking to the train, on the way to work, and all through the office hours. As the day wore on I began to feel better and better.

My colleagues at work begged me to hum something else! By about 4:00 p.m. they were nearly having a fit. So I hummed more softly. By the time I left for home the healing was almost complete.

That night my wife asked me to explain how I came to identify the cause of my problem, so I gave her the whole story. We picked a passage at random from one of the ECK works by Paul Twitchell before going to sleep. Not surprisingly, it read, "Some of the external causes that man is daily assaulted by are: music . . . "

41. The Big Match

My office usually had a lottery for one or more of the major sporting events each year. For a nominal fee, one could speculate on the outcome. I generally didn't participate, except on one occasion when I got a strong nudge to get involved.

It was a dollar a bet or three bets for two dollars. Most of my co-workers placed several bets.

I joked that I knew the result and that there was no point in my fellow workers wasting their money. They turned up their noses at my whimsy, but I placed one bet and paid a dollar.

They asked me repeatedly what I had meant by my remark, but I refused to reveal the details of my prediction. I didn't want them to use the information themselves and divide the winnings! They were a bit annoyed at my self-confidence, and we all waited for the results to be announced the following week.

Over the weekend I told my family about the prediction. It had come with such clarity. I just *knew* what the final scores would be. They too got curious about the outcome.

When the results were announced, no one was

more surprised than my office mates. My prediction was correct.

The spiritual lessons for me behind this were twofold. First, it was a needed demonstration as to how the ECK-Vidya, the ancient science of prophecy, can work. Two hundred and twenty-one bets were placed from the seventy-nine workers in the office. One reason I had had this ECK-Vidya experience was that I had no real interest in the outcome, no selfish motives.

The second lesson was about the Law of Silence. Having heard how I had made the prediction, one nervous fellow gravely accused me of using magic.

This taught me to be more discreet about revealing my inner experiences to others.

42. Reassurance

A journalist got in touch with me. Would I agree to be interviewed for an article on ECKANKAR? He said it would be part of a series on minority religions, including the Mormons, Baha'is, and other groups.

ECKists in our area were concerned about local newspaper articles on ECKANKAR that had appeared over the past years, since the articles were often full of distortions and presented the teachings in a sensational and inaccurate way.

Despite my misgivings, I agreed to be interviewed.

When the article appeared, it was awful. There were many factual inaccuracies, and it was not even part of a series. Several of us wrote the editor for a retraction, but nothing was done. I privately wondered if I had done the right thing by agreeing to the interview. Would the readers be able to extract the spiritually valid material from the journalist's sensationalized writing?

For several days after the article's publication, I felt very unsure of myself. It wasn't easy to shake off the feeling that I had let down my fellow ECKists.

At this low point, the ECK brought unexpected reassurance.

I was preparing for bed one night, debating whether I should visit a secondhand bookstore the following day. I had been searching for months for three books: a set of Graves's Claudius novels, a copy of *The Greeks* by Kitto, and Vasari's *Lives of the Artists*. Though I had been after these titles for some time, they had continued to elude me.

The despondency over the newspaper article still hung over me the next day. As I walked into the bookstore, I asked the Mahanta for positive confirmation that I had actually done the right thing in giving the interview.

In the next moment, I spied on the shelf facing me a bound set of Graves's Claudius novels. They were in excellent condition—and quite inexpensive. This really gave me a lift. The answer to my confusion, which was coming in so warm and reassuring a fashion, left me smiling broadly.

As I stood clutching the set of novels, my eyes ran across the shelves. Just then I happened to see another book I had been seeking for several months. Taking it down, I flicked through it and for some reason placed it back on the shelf.

At that very moment, a young lady entered the shop. She walked deliberately across the floor to the shelf next to me, whisked down the book I had just replaced, paid for it, and walked out. It all happened so fast that I just stared at the door. The Mahanta was giving me a gentle reproof: "Take your opportunities lest they vanish!"

Out of the corner of my eye I spotted Vasari's

Lives of the Artists. It too was in excellent condition. Well, I thought, this splendid reply to my doubts and misgivings was almost too generous. But the Mahanta was not finished yet. Turning to a set of neighboring shelves I saw at about eye level a copy of Kitto's *The Greeks.*

I began laughing aloud then. I reached up for the book, reflecting back almost eight years to when I had first studied Kitto's volume. The Mahanta, who had been silent for a while, made a quiet suggestion: "Robert, why not check inside the cover?"

My full name was there, in blue ink.

43. "Ask for Me!"

A young lady I knew wanted a healing. She had tried her doctor and several standard remedies, but nothing brought her relief. The symptoms included cyclical bouts of fatigue and almost constant muscular pain. Her condition had persisted for about six weeks and showed no signs of letting up.

Since she knew I took all my problems, including health troubles, to the Mahanta for guidance and direction, she asked me one day, "Robert, can you have a word with him?" Even if nothing came of it, she reasoned, it couldn't hurt to ask.

As she drove away in her car, she shouted through the window, lest I forget, "Ask for me! Ask for me!"

The next morning her pains were gone and her strength fully restored. The next time we saw each other, she told me about the healing. "What did you do?" she asked me.

"Nothing," I said. "I simply heard your petition and went about my business. What the Holy Spirit did about it was none of my concern. You set a new cycle in motion yourself just by having the humility to ask the Mahanta for assistance."

She looked bemused at my answer.

44. Potatoes

I felt I had to make a change in my diet, so I consulted a friend who had studied dietetics for many years. The system he advocated was to eat proteins and carbohydrates at separate meals. Everything went well in my new regime for a while, but then I began feeling weak.

I knew I needed something to improve my vitality, but oddly enough I didn't connect my poor health with my diet change.

About the same time I attended an ECKANKAR seminar. In one of his talks, the Living ECK Master spoke about Paul Twitchell's book *Herbs: The Magic Healers.*

He mentioned how some parts of the book needed updating to reflect advances in medical knowledge and that a revised edition was being worked on. He listed some of the items covered in the book. At one point I thought he said, "For example, take potatoes . . . " and paused. Instead of continuing, he went off on a different track.

A little while later in the talk I heard him say again, "Take potatoes . . . " and went off on another topic. He never got around to finishing either statement. I don't know if anyone else heard this phrase, but for some reason it caught my attention and set me wondering.

Over the following weeks the phrase "take potatoes" kept coming to mind. My health condition was not improving. If anything, it was getting worse. Then finally it dawned on me. The Mahanta was actually directing me, "Take potatoes." I had solved the problem of separating proteins and carbohydrates by cutting down on the latter. Potatoes had disappeared from my diet. This was not good for me.

As soon as I added potatoes back in, my health quickly returned to normal.

This experience taught me a valuable lesson about well-meaning advice. Whether we listen is entirely our own responsibility. Right discrimination is a most valuable asset on the path home to God.

Chapter Six

The Swans of God

45. A Big Step

Early in 1984 I received the pink slip for the Fourth Initiation. This is a notice of eligibility from the Living ECK Master that I was ready to take the next major step in my spiritual unfoldment. It was a lovely surprise.

The ECK had given me a tip shortly before the envelope arrived. An ECKist living in a remote region of the country had sent me a lovingly hand-drawn and colored notecard of a white dove descending with a five-pointed gold leaf in its beak. This gave outer confirmation that the Fourth Initiation was a big step for me toward the Fifth Circle—toward becoming one of the Brothers of the Leaf.

In a similar way, I received another tip from the ECK slightly before my Fifth Initiation. I was in a cab heading for the airport, en route to an ECKANKAR seminar. Riding with me was an elderly Canadian couple. The woman chatted amiably about their special trip which they had greatly enjoyed.

Then her husband, who had been silent all this time, suddenly leaned forward and offered me a maple-leaf pin. He said nothing, just smiled. I accepted his gift.

A few weeks after this happened I received my secret word for the Fifth Circle through the inner channels. Then the pink slip for the Fifth Initiation arrived in the mail about two months later.

46. New Shoes

Some weeks after I entered the Fourth Circle, I set off to buy a new pair of shoes. The old ones were falling apart, and I figured it was time for a change. My shopping trip took me to several stores across town.

After trying on dozens of pairs, I finally made a choice. The whole process took a long time, but it was worth it to have a pair of shoes that fit.

After just a few days, my new shoes began to feel very uncomfortable. My calves hurt when I walked. Maybe the heels were too high. The cobbler reheeled them, but now they sent a thud up my spine with each step.

The pain continued, so I returned to the cobbler and had a set of softer heels fitted. These too were uncomfortable, but I wore them anyway—at least until the discomfort became unbearable. Finally I decided there was no option but to buy another pair of shoes.

The whole saga began again. After visiting about ten stores and trying on dozens of pairs of shoes, I found one pair that would fit. With so much experience behind me, I felt sure I couldn't possibly get it wrong this time.

But I did. After a few days this second pair began causing problems. I reduced the height of the heels with an electric sander, but they still weren't right. A lift placed inside each shoe didn't help either.

It wasn't until some years later that I realized my experience with the ill-fitting shoes had to do with my experience in the Fourth Circle. Each circle of initiation in ECKANKAR carries a whole new experience in the Light and Sound. It's as if we're learning afresh the entire spectrum of the spiritual laws.

Soul struggles over many lifetimes to learn these laws and find a spiritual state which fits perfectly. Like pairs of shoes, many options are tried, but none are quite right.

The shoe saga lasted all through my Fourth Initiation. It was not until I entered the Fifth Circle that I found a pair that were truly comfortable.

47. Swans

When I was six years old, I was very fond of a television program which dramatized a different fairy tale each week. During one particular episode, I was lifted into a glorious state of consciousness that lasted for almost an hour.

The fairy tale was about swans. Though I had little understanding of what was actually happening, the joy almost overwhelmed me.

The Paramhansas of the Soul Plane, the swans of God radiant with the light of heaven, are mentioned in the ECK writings. That afternoon, long before I had read about them, the images of swans on the screen became the Paramhansas of the Soul Plane.

Though I watched the program without fail for several months, yearning for a repeat of the Soul Plane experience, nothing happened. But this and similar adventures in the Soul body spurred me to find the Living ECK Master in later life.

About two years prior to my Fifth Initiation, an ECKist I corresponded with sent me a small painting of a graceful swan. It gave me quiet reassurance that I had taken a significant step in the direction of the Fifth Plane, where live the swans of God.

The Fifth Initiation was what opened that door once more.

48. Guide for the Perplexed

I had run into an unsolvable problem concerning two friends who were unreconcilable. The inner guidance said that it was important for me to hang in there. But beyond that, no further insights came. I had to trust the Mahanta to reveal what I needed to know in good time.

As the days passed I felt more and more uneasy. I finally decided to relax one afternoon by browsing through a favorite bookstore. As I walked in, I asked inwardly, "Well, Mahanta, what is going on? What am I failing to see?" I was prepared to accept the most unlikely reply, provided it got to the bottom of things.

I crossed to the nearest shelf and absently took down a volume. My attention was still on the Mahanta. As I opened the book at random, my mouth fell open in surprise. While one page was in English, the other was printed in a strange alphabet that I had never seen before.

As I examined the strange page, I realized that the text was English, but actually printed as a mirror image, probably due to a printing error. The Mahanta was presenting a clue to my problem. Just as the reversed type would only become readable if held to a mirror, I would only be able to make sense of what was happening by flipping over, or reversing, my viewpoint.

With this new insight, everything became obvious: My problem was an illusion. I need do nothing.

I closed the book to check the title and was again surprised. It read *A Guide for the Perplexed* by E. F. Schumacher. Seeing that it had held so many clues, I decided to buy it. After all, the Mahanta might not be finished using it.

When I got home, something nudged me to examine the odd page again. Using a mirror I read the first few lines: "The higher the Level of Being, the greater is the importance of inner experience, i.e. the 'inner life', as compared with outer appearances."

As if this weren't enough, a little farther down it read: "Let us then begin with other people. How do we gain knowledge of what is going on inside them? As I have said before, we are living in a world of *invisible* people; most of them do not even wish us to know anything about their inner life; they say, 'Don't intrude, leave me alone, mind your own business.'"

Having gotten this excellent guidance on how to handle my problem with my two friends, I followed it. Not long after, they resolved their dispute with a simple solution that satisfied everyone.

49. Pearl of Heaven

When I arrived home on my birthday and found the pink slip for the Fifth Initiation in the mailbox, I had to sit down to steady myself.

In a sense it hardly seemed possible. To calm my excitement, I sipped some tea and glanced through the evening paper. But it was a futile exercise as nothing I read seemed to register.

My thoughts raced back to the time, several thousand years ago, when I had last received the high initiation from the Living ECK Master. In that incarnation I had blown my golden opportunity. Arrogance and vanity proved my undoing. I thought I knew more than God's chosen vehicle, the Mahanta, the Living ECK Master.

With the arrival of this pink slip, I was being offered the opportunity once again.

Then the Golden-tongued Wisdom spoke, encapsulating the essence of this golden moment. My attention focused on a cartoon column in the newspaper. It seemed to shine from the page. Through its simple story the Mahanta embraced me with the deepest compassion.

The cartoon strip was in three parts. The first showed a possum, Fossil, and a dog, Toby, both hanging by their tails from a tree branch. Fossil was showing Toby how to hang by his tail.

"That's great, Toby," he said. "I've finally taught you how to do it. Wonderful."

Then as Fossil started to say, "But don't," Toby fell, landing on his head with a painful "whumph!" Fossil completed the warning, "wag your tail!"

This made me laugh so much I forgot my nervousness. The Mahanta was reminding me to hold steady this time. With a spiritual hug, he was saying, "That's great, Robert. I've finally taught you how to do it. Wonderful—but don't wag your tail!"

When you work really hard for the pearl of heaven, giving everything you have to secure this sacred goal, there comes a time when you forget all about the whole process, the growth and change, and simply be.

When I first stepped on the path of ECK in August 1975, I asked Fubbi Quantz how long it would take before I became spiritually free.

"Thirty years," he replied.

At the time, I didn't mind—thirty years didn't seem so long for all that was being sought.

One day in 1986 it struck me that what Fubbi had said was amazingly accurate. I received the pink slip for the Fifth Initiation on my thirtieth birthday.

Chapter Seven

Secret Teachings

50. Listen!

Being prone to getting lost in my thoughts and sometimes jumping to conclusions, I wasn't too good at listening. This is a spiritual art, one which is essential to our progress in ECKANKAR.

Having just entered the Fifth Circle, there was definitely a lot for me to learn. It seemed the real work was only just beginning. My spiritual chemistry lacked the humility to simply listen. So the Mahanta gave me many lessons, some subtle, some quite direct. All to no avail. I wasn't getting the message. So something more effective was needed.

A staff member in my office became very uncooperative. We were on completely different wavelengths. He became convinced I wasn't listening to his real needs—and perhaps I wasn't. My boss was so struck by the bad feelings in the office one afternoon that he called me to his private office. This was serious.

We sat at his table, and he slowly began to speak. I was the worst communicator he had ever met, the worst manager he had ever come across. No matter who worked for me, they were bound to suffer.

"You must learn to listen, Robert! You must learn to listen!" He went on and on like this, and all the time I had to hold my hand over my mouth to keep from laughing. The Mahanta was getting the message across loud and clear!

A few weeks later I was asked by the Living ECK Master to serve as an ECK Spiritual Aide, a sacred responsibility that requires the skill of listening. I guess I must have gotten the message.

My boss later apologized. He said he didn't know what had come over him.

51. The Principles of God

On the weekend after my Fifth Initiation, a man knocked on my front door. He was selling raffle tickets for charity. When I offered to buy one, he jotted down the number of our house in his receipt book, muttering as he did so, "131."

"Yes, 131," I confirmed.

He then looked up at the number on our door and exclaimed, "No, it's 130!"

He was right. Why did I say 131?

The next day I went to a dining club for lunch. A fellow at the door was accepting membership renewals. I filled out a form and collected my new membership card.

There was the same number again—131.

It wasn't until the following day that I realized the message the Mahanta was giving me with this recurring number. At the ECK Center a new Second Initiate asked me to help him find the part in *The Shariyat-Ki-Sugmad,* Book One, where it talks about the three principles of ECK and the one overall principle.

When I looked up the reference at home, it was

on page 131 in the first edition of the book. I knew that these principles were of great importance to my spiritual growth:

1. Soul is always in eternity
2. Soul is in the present, not in the future and not in the past
3. Soul is always in the heavenly state of God

The overall principle was: Soul exists because God wills it.

Since I had just recently joined the Fifth Circle, the Mahanta was telling me it was necessary to review these vital principles of the spiritual life.

Several months later I got a renewed nudge to contemplate again on the three principles of ECK and the overall principle. Thoughts of their dynamics had been stirring in my mind for days. When this happens I know the Inner Master wants me to probe more deeply into a subject, to let the essence of the precept enter more fully into my consciousness.

That evening I relaxed to Prokofiev's seventh symphony. To my ears, this lovely composition represents Soul's upward journey into the high planes of God. This set me thinking once more about the basic principle of ECK. As I removed the record from the turntable, I finally put my question to the Mahanta directly:

"Well, Wah Z, are these three principles truly vital to my spiritual growth?"

Just then my eye fell on the opus number for this sublime piece of music. It was 131.

52. Love or Crumble

While at a business seminar, I noticed a knot of tension growing inside me. It had become so tight that I felt sure a deep crisis was brewing. The anxiety was extreme.

I sat down to do a contemplation when I recognized the voice of the Mahanta speaking to me. I realized that some of his remarks were from the ECK writings. But I had never heard this spiritual law expressed so firmly.

"Love or crumble," he said. "The razor's edge is the fine line between self-service and service to God. It is love, and love alone, that unifies these four truths: the razor's edge, the love which is the fine unbreakable thread, the fine line between the human consciousness and God Consciousness, and the fine line of communication between the Mahanta and the student."

Pausing to look me carefully in the eye, he said again, "Love or crumble."

This little discourse hit the nail on the head. The Master was showing me how I had been missing the essence of the spiritual works.

With this vital principle to remind me, I quickly regained my inner composure.

53. Oranges

One evening in contemplation I found myself in the Temple of Namayatan, the main Temple of Golden Wisdom on the Mental Plane. The building was huge inside. Standing next to me was the ECK Master Paul Twitchell, dressed in a light blue shirt and dark blue slacks. Smiling, he sat down on, of all things, an empty orange crate. What a strange seat, I thought.

"How are things?" he asked, looking up at me.

"Sometimes, Paul, I wonder," I replied.

"Well, you're here," he said. I guessed that was something.

"Where would you like to go?" he continued. Since we were in the main Temple of Golden Wisdom on the Mental Plane, I said I'd like to look around. "Fine," he replied.

We walked down a wide corridor. The walls were a clouded glass, with stainless-steel ribbing. Walking some distance, we arrived at what seemed like a junction of several passageways. To our left was a darkened corridor. I asked Paul why it was unlit. "They are renovating that wing," he answered.

"Instead of putting up signs, they just turn out the lights. Works better." I thought that sounded very sensible.

As Paul and I approached a smaller corridor, a tall, lean man emerged from an elevator right next to me.

"I'd like you to meet Ori Diogo," said Paul. The tall ECK Master wore a long white robe. His hair was longish and black, and he had a black beard. He smiled at me and bowed slightly, extending his hand.

Paul left us as I followed Ori Diogo up an escalator. There was no one else in the area. We went up several flights of stairs; I thought if we went any higher we'd be through the roof by now. And that's where we emerged, into a large, bright expanse of carefully cultivated orange trees. They were everywhere.

The ECK Master still said nothing but simply walked down a long row between the trees. I followed.

As we went along I wondered what this whole experience was about. Why had Ori Diogo not spoken? Then I got to thinking: The ECK Masters often teach by bringing us on a little tour so that we can learn by observation.

As soon as I thought that, the ECK Master spoke. "That is it precisely!" he said. "The chela must learn to see the hand of God in the smallest things. It takes love to do this." His voice was broken and musical, rather unusual.

"Look at these orange trees," he continued, pointing. "Can you tell them apart? The man who planted them can. He cares for them and loves them." I could see now the connection between the orange grove and the empty orange crate which Paul had used as a seat.

Ori Diogo continued, "The man who tends this grove can even tell which tree yielded which oranges." At this point I must have raised my eyebrows, because he said emphatically, "Does this seem impossible? He can do this because the training, discipline, and love have ripened within him a fine faculty for discrimination."

This experience was pointing out to me the need to develop the capacity to see the presence of God in the smallest and most ordinary things. My recent restlessness was caused by not having the love within to be content with here and now. When there is no pushing to be elsewhere, this makes for contentment and inner peace.

As if reading my thoughts again, Ori Diogo smiled at me and finished, "The student's hunger for God will always open new doors."

54. Magpie, Badger, and Fox

A few months after entering the Fifth Circle, I received a letter from a new ECKist who was having problems coming to terms with ECKANKAR.

His family believed that he had left the Catholic religion to adopt what was, in their eyes, a pagan path. To shake his newfound faith, they had given him a copy of a magazine devoted entirely to debunking ECKANKAR and Paul Twitchell.

This was not an easy test for the young man. When a seemingly objective journalist presents "facts" in a certain way, the reader's judgment can be easily influenced. It can also be a trial simply because the reasons behind a Master's actions are not always easy to perceive.

Our common sense should play a role in all of this. Yet a clever writer can be very effective in distorting the true state of affairs: a slant here, a bias there, and—presto!—illusion.

After reading the magazine myself I thought, How can I give this young man a clear reply? No matter what I say, he will still need to make the judgment himself. Uncertain as to how I should proceed, I asked the Mahanta for guidance.

The following morning I set off to buy a tree as a gift for a friend. Since there was only one dealer locally who maintains consistently good stock, I headed straight for Mr. Watson's nursery.

As I entered the extensive gardens, I passed a fellow coming out with a fine sapling under his arm— a weeping willow. This reminded me of Paul Twitchell and the gentle experiences he had recorded in his poetic book *Stranger by the River.* I thought of how this ECK Master took truth where he found it, polished it up, and having renewed its vitality, offered it to the world in a way his readers could understand.

Going across to the office, I found Mr. Watson in a talkative mood. He seemed to lapse into reverie and speak from within himself. What could have set him off? Perhaps the ECK would use him to convey the Golden-tongued Wisdom I needed badly?

He began by telling me about a family of badgers that used to live where our home now stood. Badgers were much maligned creatures, he said. Because they are seldom seen, people suppose they are up to no good. In reality, though, they are very clean and orderly animals, never soiling their nests (or sets). Diligent and gifted diggers, they excavate marvelous chambers in the earth.

Mr. Watson added, "The fox, however, arrives on the scene and soils the set, leaving his droppings and scattering animal carcasses about. In comparison with the badger, the fox is a very dirty animal indeed. The badger can't live in that kind of environment and must leave when the fox makes his home nearby. The stink is more than the badger can bear.

"The fox is unable to dig his own set, and so he lazily relies on the badger to do this for him. When the local people see the carcasses of lambs in and around the set, they mistakenly blame the badger, when in reality it is the fox that is responsible."

That's interesting, I thought. The ECK Masters cut out pathways in the lower worlds for seekers of truth. When these pathways become soiled, the ECK Masters move on and the foxes take over.

Mr. Watson went on to talk about the local magpies, who had shown extraordinary initiative. Entering his large greenhouse, they had foraged about until they located the store of hard biscuits reserved exclusively for Mr. Watson's cats.

"For the magpies," he said, "the biscuits are indigestible. So they dropped them in the cats' milk and flew to a nearby tree. After about fifteen minutes, they returned and retrieved the softened biscuits."

This also reminded me of Paul Twitchell, taking truth where he found it and rendering it into a form digestible by the seeker.

Pointing to the trees, Mr. Watson said the rooks were now building their nests. This meant the really hard weather had passed and while we might still have a few spells of frost and cold, there would be no more biting winds to contend with. Knowing the good trees from the bad, the rooks wouldn't build their nests in unsafe places. Even though they may all look the same to the untrained eye, the rooks knew which trees were sturdy and which would fall in a storm.

The ECK was giving such a vivid reply to the chela's question that I simply stared in amazement at Mr. Watson.

He wasn't finished. The insects, he said, will go on and on. "While mammals come and go," he said, "becoming extinct, the insects remain. We may not see them, but they are there. They haven't changed in millions of years; they seem immutable." To me, this was a reference to the ECK Itself—invisible, immutable, eternal.

Gazing up at the birds, he continued, "They know when the really bad weather has passed. And with animals too, there is the struggle to survive. Only the fit get to mate, only the fit find food when it's scarce. They have to work harder but they are better able to survive than the weak. It's a struggle."

He paused. "That's how they learn, and it's how we learn. The little child—someone steals his pen in school, he learns. You get beaten up, you learn. You fall and cut your knee, you hurt yourself, you learn. You're stronger for it."

* * *

When I got home my wife noticed our license plate had fallen off the front of the car. Our vehicle had no "label." To properly identify it, one would have to look behind at the rear license plate.

What was Divine Spirit saying in all of this? Simply that one cannot jump to a superficial understanding of ECKANKAR. We can grasp it only with our hearts, from the depths of our own experience. Surface knowledge and labels are not enough.

The day's messages were for both me and the new ECKist who had written to me: The secret teachings of the heart are revealed to those who look to the Mahanta with humility and love.

Chapter Eight

The Golden Child

55. Inner Academy

The year I was asked to be a RESA, some of the lessons I was learning were fairly demanding. RESA stands for Regional ECK Spiritual Aide, the official representative of the Living ECK Master in a designated country or state.

During my first year as RESA the Mahanta taught me a very valuable lesson in the dream state.

In the dream, about seventy of us were in one of a series of large rooms. The building was a school, and we as RESAs constituted one of its many classes. We each had our respective jobs to perform, but not everybody applied themselves fully. Instead, some seemed to feel that the good times could be enjoyed and the need for exertion wasn't so great.

Then the Master arrived with a couple of close associates. He began to ask us about our work. Everyone knew instinctively that the visit was not a social one. The whole group became very attentive.

The Master asked some individuals what they had been doing, in a way which made it clear that they had been neglecting their duties as RESAs. When they tried to give answers that would conceal their laziness, the Master grew extremely stern.

His expression became intent, and he asked some very probing questions. Clearly, these individuals thought they could get off the hook by giving plausible answers, but this wasn't so. The Master pursued each reply to its full conclusion. Nothing could be hidden.

I was taken aback by the Master's severity. I had never seen him like this before. Each of us in the group was totally accountable for all our actions as RESA. There was no possibility of anyone evading this fact. We were accountable—not just in a vague, mystical way but publicly, in very concrete terms. Were we or were we not attending to the tasks given to us, and doing them to the very best of our abilities? Our schooling was neither a game nor an honor.

The Master's approach shocked me so much it felt like I was standing on ground struck by lightning. This reminded me of *svaha,* a word Sri Harold had once used to describe the interval between two events, such as the lightning flash and the clap of thunder. For the RESA, the storm is directly overhead. The comforting interval between the lightning and thunder is nil.

The schooling we were receiving was in a huge academy, like a military academy, with the same high levels of discipline and obedience. We were like second graders in a vast establishment that ran up to fifteen or twenty grades. Those who graduated were Vairagi Adepts.

To be a member of the academy was not just an honor. It demanded all our effort, attention, and dedication. Those who fell below minimum standards—even fractionally—were immediately expelled. We were each totally accountable to the supreme commander, the Mahanta, for the least of our actions. There was no middle ground. No room for self-indulgence.

As Paul Twitchell said, we are completely for the ECK or we are against It. The experience of that schoolroom shook me into a new awareness of what it means to serve the Mahanta as a Regional ECK Spiritual Aide.

56. Writing on the Wall

While digging in the front garden one after-noon, I had to put up with loud, discordant rock music from a nearby alleyway. A group of teen-agers were gathered. Finally when I could stand it no longer, I walked across and asked them to move on.

I was prepared to discuss our respective points of view. But the youngsters were exceptionally rude. One especially caught me off balance, and I used a few salty words to wake him up.

This must have worked. Not long after I went back to my gardening the music stopped.

As I resumed digging, I wondered if I had been as neutral as I could have. The teens had their space too. Perhaps my choice of words could have been more generous, I mused. Still it was all water under the bridge—or so I thought.

The group never returned, but a few days later, while walking through the alleyway, I happened to see my salty expression sprayed in green paint all along the wall.

I was learning that my past actions had a way

of catching up to me very fast now. The farther we travel along the spiritual path, the quicker the return. At times it can be almost instantaneous.

57. Royal Mile

During a vacation to Scotland in June 1987, my wife and I took a trip to Edinburgh one rainy morning. Our itinerary began with the John Knox House. It stood on a grand thoroughfare known as the Royal Mile.

This rugged and unruly founder of Scottish Presbyterianism lived a life in conflict with the Catholic monarch, Mary, Queen of Scots, trying to win her over to his own brand of Christianity.

As we left Knox's house and walked up the Royal Mile toward the castle, the rain stopped. The sun shone brilliantly on the stonework and cobbled street. I noticed a large throng of people, mostly tourists, lining the sidewalk. We learned that the queen of England was due to pass shortly. My wife decided to wait.

Having no interest in the royal family and preferring instead to stay cool, I sheltered in an elevated archway out of the sun. This proved to be a surprisingly good location. When the queen did ride by in her maroon Rolls-Royce, I had a perfect view.

As the Rolls glided past, the queen waved up at

149

me. I felt like an idiot until I heard the Mahanta whisper, "And that breaks your final link with the past."

This took me completely by surprise. Did I once have a link to the monarchy? It wasn't until later that I realized the connection.

Working out karma from past lives can be a very interesting experience. Sometimes the Mahanta will show us a long-forgotten incident or attachment which gave rise to a condition that is now troubling us. This had occurred several years before when I went through a period of illness and a very difficult spell of working off past karma.

Gradually it was revealed to me in dreams that I had been Protestant in past lives. In order to rebalance a lot of fixed opinions, I incarnated as a Roman Catholic this time. It compelled me to face certain facts about myself. It also allowed me to clean out a lot of past misconceptions.

Some of the karma that was wound up on that Edinburgh visit related to earlier lives in England and Scotland. Following the Reformation, religion had been very closely related to politics in those countries. The king or queen were believed by many to possess divine rights, certain transcendental qualities.

In order to release some old Protestant attitudes which were still embedded in my subconscious mind, the Mahanta quietly arranged that I revisit the past.

58. Lump of Coal

After attending an ECKANKAR introductory talk, my wife and I came out to discover our car was missing. Rather than get upset, we calmly contacted the police, reported the details, and took the train home. The next day the police found the car, and my wife went to pick it up.

The thieves had gotten inside the vehicle by smashing the front passenger window with a lump of coal. The coal was still on the seat regarded as mine, since my wife usually drove. Later we made a list of everything that had been stolen as well as a complete inventory of the contents of the car. I knew the ECK was speaking through this unusual event, and I wanted to record all the details.

The following items were missing: my wife's ten-speed bicycle, a set of road maps, a package of food, a portable tape player, the car jack, and an old, stained pink blanket. Left behind were sunglasses, four tires, and the spare.

The lists answered a great deal for me at the time. The stolen items were pieces in a mosaic that was finally taking shape. The break-in itself represented a breakthrough in spiritual growth. The lump of coal on my seat was frozen energy, energy that would be released later when I could handle it. This breakthrough was matched by an unusual incident the morning of the theft.

I had been sitting at my desk at work when I felt a small explosion behind my Spiritual Eye. It startled me so much I felt I was about to leave this world. But the fireworks abated. After about an hour I felt recovered enough to make my way home unassisted.

Our old maps were taken; new inner maps were now needed. Fresh supplies of food would be required since our food had been taken. The tape player for the outer ears was but a crude reflection of the inner sounds, the Music of ECK. The jack was no longer needed because the vehicle, the spiritual consciousness, was already uplifted. Finally, the loss of the stained pink blanket showed that the Astral, or emotional, level of experience had been cleaned out.

The items that remained also told a story. The sunglasses would come in handy as a protection against the stronger Light. The four tires and a spare indicated mobility, that continued good use would be made of the vehicle.

This waking dream was a major source of support to me during a very difficult period in my life. Using the ECK-Vidya, the Mahanta was giving me survival tips for the future. I found the stamina and determination to persist and prepare for what was to come.

59. The Golden Child

The Year of Spiritual Healing, which techni-
cally began on October 22, 1985, caught up
with me during 1987. About three months before
illness struck, I had a series of unusual dream
messages. On March 5 I recorded:

> I was a famous singer who went everywhere
> with his little golden-haired baby. I wasn't sure
> whether the baby was male or female. Photogra-
> phers swarmed to take our photos. I put a stop to
> this since I didn't want the baby treated as an
> object. Later, I fell into bad ways and lost the child
> to an orphanage. Things got so bad that I was
> about to take my life. I went into the woods with
> my rifle, but I had a change of heart at the last
> moment. Leaving the woods I went to the orphan-
> age, but the staff there couldn't believe I was the
> same person (the baby's father). A few years had
> elapsed. I at least managed to get them to let me
> work nearby on menial chores.

The prophetic significance of the dream eluded
me. The Dream Master gave me several more related messages during the next few weeks. Looking

back, I see now that the following three dreams were most important:

March 12, 1987: I was selling insurance. The insurance was twenty dollars for twelve years in ECKANKAR.

March 16, 1987: I was with the Mahanta and another RESA in an office. While we were taking some papers from a file cabinet, Wah Z brought my attention to the fact that the top of my head, from above the ears and all around, was glowing white. He asked me what we called this at home. I said we called it the Mahanta's Cap or some such name. He laughed at this reply and good-naturedly said, 'Sure, any name will do, as Lewis Carroll says!' I was struck by Wah Z's radiance, joy, and love.

March 19, 1987: I was asked if I wanted the Sixth Initiation. I replied that I felt there was a great deal yet to learn in the Fifth.

These dreams were clearly pointing to a spiritual change of great importance, but due to my immaturity I couldn't quite identify what this was.

On April 22 I decided to set a date for God-Realization. The ECK Master Paul Twitchell told the story many times in public talks of his date with God-Realization. He spoke of how he lay on his bed at the prescribed time, waiting for the great illumination to hit him. But nothing happened. He was very disappointed.

A few weeks after the specified date, however, it struck him out of the blue.

The date and time I set were June 15 at 7:00 a.m. As I did this, the Mahanta asked, "Are you sure this is what you want, Robert?" I knew from the way the

Master put the question that there could be pain and troubles ahead.

Pausing for a moment, I replied, "Well, I'll have to face it sometime." The Master made no reply.

Two weeks later, on May 6, my health failed. My entire body was overcome by a great tiredness. My eyes were so disturbed I was unable to read. This all seemed to be the result of overworking.

The fatigue gradually lifted after a few weeks' rest, but my eyes showed no improvement. A specialist could find no organic weaknesses. Yet there was a knot behind my eyes, a bundle of tension in the area of my Spiritual Eye. For ten weeks I was unable to do any reading whatsoever. Other than that I was in good health.

June 15 came and went. Nothing seemed to have happened.

Then on July 12, it felt as if the knot at my Spiritual Eye had dissolved and drained down through my entire body. I became quite ill. I was concerned that I would miss the ECK European Seminar in Holland that same week. On July 15 I struggled to get to the airport, unsure whether I should be going at all. That morning the Mahanta had said with deep compassion, "Robbie, good will."

At first I delayed checking in at the airport. Then I checked in and minutes later checked out. With only seconds left, I checked in again and ran down the ramp. I was the last passenger to board; the crew were waiting for me. They could see I was struggling, and they didn't rush me. But try as I might, I just couldn't take that step into the cabin of the plane.

So I turned back. It was the hardest step I've ever taken.

The doctors diagnosed my illness as potentially serious. They said they would have to watch it for a few weeks to be certain. If they were right I might never work again.

The turmoil and disorientation were dreadful. So many shocks at once increased the burden I felt. All the disasters I thought could never happen were in the process of exploding: loss of health, job, income, even my wife, home, and friends.

In that greatly weakened state, these were all imminent realities. I had no defense against them. The most cutting sadness of all was the belief that I had let down the Mahanta, the Living ECK Master. Maybe I would never be well enough again to serve in this physical world.

What had I done? Why had I made a premature bid for God-Realization? What foolishness had possessed me?

The love of the Mahanta supported me throughout this trial. Everything else was gone.

A few days later I asked Wah Z, "Why am I going through this *now?*" He gave an immediate reply: "Look ahead eleven days."

This didn't seem to make any sense. What was so significant about August 1? Then I remembered: It was the twelfth anniversary of the day I joined ECKANKAR.

Every twelve years or so we may undergo a chemical change to reflect our inner spiritual transformation. The dream on March 12 was now making sense: "insurance for twelve years in ECKANKAR."

Right up to July 31 the illness bit deeply and caused a great deal of pain and turmoil. But the following morning, August 1, I felt considerably better. A great weight had lifted. The healing had begun. I thanked the Mahanta from the depths of my heart.

Later that afternoon I went on a celebratory bike ride along a coastal road. This was my first trip outside my home in over two weeks. As I went down the hill and approached the tunnel, the Mahanta gave me a nudge: "A message is coming. Watch for it."

Having gone through the tunnel, I stood on the far side waiting for some traffic to pass. A little boy came up to me. He had beautiful golden hair, sparkling blue eyes, and a full round face. He wore a blue-and-white striped T-shirt.

Though he could have been no more than four, he was surprisingly confident before a stranger. Looking me straight in the eye he said in a loud, clear voice, "Your bike's a great bike!" I knew then that the ECK was speaking through this little child. This whole episode was a waking dream to compliment the dream I had had on March 5. This was the golden-haired child I had lost to the orphanage.

Then the child pointed to the gear shifter on the handlebar and asked, "What's that for?" Laughing I told him. The joy of ECK was flooding through me now. The child was the handsomest I had ever seen. Looking around, I saw his mother with a companion. Their dress was so dowdy and drab that it seemed at first they might be gypsies. Immediately I thought, travelers.

My heart soared. I had come through the tunnel.

My vehicle, the bike, represented my physical body and was "great." And I was being gently reminded never again to strive for too much all at once. After all, what are gears for?

God-Realization would come in its own good time. And most of all, the golden child, the living truth of ECK, was with me and within me.

Chapter Nine

Spiritual Marriage

60. Old Habits

In the summer of 1988, I got clear direction from the Mahanta to switch to a new restaurant for my midday meal. The food in my favorite diner was no longer suited to my state of consciousness. So, after nine years of frequenting the same place almost every day, it was time for a change.

But change wasn't easy. I tried a few alternate restaurants, none of which proved satisfactory. Mentally shrugging my shoulders, I returned to my familiar haunt. Old habits die hard.

A few weeks later the restaurant owners informed me that they would be closing. This was a bolt from the blue. They had been in service for over thirty years! No one could quite believe the place was going out of business. It had become such a local legend that some of the more elderly patrons were even interviewed on national radio.

When my wife heard what had happened, she remarked, "Now look what you've done! Because you wouldn't change, the ECK closed the place down. Now you *must* change!"

61. Protection

While my wife drove me home from work one evening, I listened attentively as she told a story. She became so engrossed in it herself that her attention wasn't fully on the road ahead.

The Mahanta spoke softly: "Watch the car in front." It was towing a trailer with a large lawnmower inside.

A little while later, the soft inner voice came again: "Keep watching it, Robert. The trailer is going to collapse in five seconds." I counted.

The instant the trailer collapsed, I called to my wife, "Slow down! Slow down!" She immediately slammed on the brakes.

Without the timely inner tip, we could have crashed into the trailer.

The ECK Masters state that the working of Divine Spirit in our lives is often most evident in small details, not necessarily in grand events.

62. Rotten Apple

I came home from work one day with a problem weighing heavily on my mind. A friend had been unkind, or so it seemed. Should I ignore the matter or bring it up as an issue to be resolved?

After dwelling on the problem for about half an hour, I asked the Mahanta for advice. As I did so, I opened the refrigerator door for some margarine. My eyes fell on a strange object hidden behind the tub of margarine—a completely rotten apple!

How did that get there? I wondered.

As I threw the black ball into the garbage, I made the connection. An old lump of karma was being cleaned from my life just like that piece of rotten fruit.

With this realization, the weight inside me lifted immediately.

63. Co-worker

One night in the dream state I met Wah Z, the Mahanta. We sat at a long wooden table in one of the larger Temples of Golden Wisdom.

There had been so much happening in my inner and outer life, such a rich harvest of experiences. I warmly thanked the Mahanta for allowing me to have so many valuable lessons and spiritual adventures.

He smiled and said, "Robert, they are my experiences too, you know."

This didn't make sense at the time. Back in the waking state, I mulled it over. The depth of the Mahanta's reply gradually became clear. We think we walk the path for our own benefit, alone, unfolding over time on the journey to God.

But when we live within the protective mantle of the Living ECK Master, we are unfolding for the Mahanta as well and uplifting all Souls under his care. In a sense, God is learning more about ITSELF through each one of us.

We are individuals, but we are also Co-workers. The two cannot exist separately.

64. The Ease of Soul Travel

The Mahanta once gave me an amusing demonstration of how easy Soul Travel can be once we learn to let Divine Spirit have Its way, regardless.

Just after going into contemplation I found myself in an underground tunnel leading to the Temple of Golden Wisdom in Arhirit on the Etheric Plane. The glasslike towers of the building rose above us as we approached an entrance located a little below ground level.

By my side walked an ECK Master from another planet. He was a little under five feet tall with a large egg-shaped head. His face, though alien in earth terms, was soft and pleasant to behold.

As we walked along the green lattice stonework beneath a long archway, I reflected upon the ease with which Soul can consciously leave the body once the necessary preparations have been made. This intrigued me, so I put a question to the ECK Master at my side:

"Master, why do we so often make Soul Travel seem impossibly difficult?"

He didn't reply. I wasn't even sure he had heard my question.

A few minutes later, I heard a steady metallic thumping sound approaching from behind us. Looking around, I was surprised to see a huge green frog hopping along on a pogo stick. He had a very serious appearance and was dressed in a formal suit.

He looked so out of place, so comical, that I had to restrain myself from laughing. Paying no heed to us at all, he just went pong-ponging past. The sound of his pogo stick echoed a little in the tunnel. In a short while, he was out of sight.

What was that all about? I asked myself. And then the answer came to me.

The ECK Master *had* replied to my question. He had used this very amusing scene to show me that, when we see a dozen obstacles and barriers to Soul Travel, we are like the frog which thinks it needs a pogo stick to hop from one place to another!

65. Decisions

I had planned a two-week study leave, but I had misgivings about the timing. As I sat on the busy train headed for home that evening, the question kept revolving in my mind.

Finally I asked the Mahanta, "Do these misgivings mean I am not to take my planned study leave? I've done all I can to understand this problem. Please give me a clear sign as to what I should do."

Just then my attention was drawn to a father and son seated next to me. The boy had just lifted his comic book to show the father a page. From the graphics on the cover, I could see it was a war comic. But from where I sat the boy's hand covered the illustration. I could only make out one word as he held up the page: *Suicide.*

Then I understood: It would be suicide to take my planned study leave right now.

The ECK wasn't finished. It made quite sure I got the message. The boy quickly turned the comic; now the reverse side was visible.

It was a drawn sword.

The next morning I canceled my proposed study leave. It proved to be a wise decision.

66. Bird of Heaven

Our pair of parakeets seldom came out of their cage, and when they did they spent most of their time exploring its roof and sides. One room was their universe. I had tried bringing them out into the back garden one afternoon, but they almost went berserk from too much light and space.

One cold morning at the onset of winter, I went over to their cage to give them their daily lettuce leaf. I was a bit late for work and had already put on my overcoat and hat.

As I leaned toward the cage, the two birds froze in horror, their feathers squeezing tightly against their little bodies and their unblinking eyes bulging. What on earth was the matter with these friendly creatures? I wondered.

I made another move toward the cage, and they began flying madly against the wire walls. It was only when I backed away that they settled down, eyeing me suspiciously.

Suddenly I guessed what had unnerved them: They had never seen me wearing a hat before!

The human consciousness is just like a parakeet.

It resents change, fears the unknown. The Spiritual Exercises of ECK release the bird of heaven within each of us.

67. As If

In contemplation one day, I was greeted by the ECK Master Paul Twitchell. He wore a white shirt, open at the neck. Suspenders held up a pair of old-fashioned trousers that went a good way up the waist. Smiling, he extended a hand. "Hello, Robert," he said.

I was brimming with expectancy, eager to see where the ECK Master would take me.

Since I have no interest in fast cars, I was taken aback when Paul brought me to a racetrack. A sports car awaited me. He told me to get in, indicating that I would be driving in the next race.

After I put on the racing gear, I squeezed into the narrow seat. Leaning over, Paul asked me if I knew what to do. Intuitively I shot back, "Expand my attention to embrace the car!" He nodded. He clearly liked fast cars and was eager to see how the race would develop.

The ECK Master said I was to get above what was happening. "Drive as though the race were over," he added. I felt I understood what he meant.

The race went surprisingly well for me. Getting

above the track, I watched the cars closest to my own. This gave me the edge since I knew where to maneuver, when to accelerate, and how to dodge difficulties. After twenty closely contested laps, I came in first. Paul looked pleased.

His job finished, he handed me over to another ECK Master for the second part of the lesson.

This Asian ECK Master was shorter than Paul, with a round, plain face. He took me to a small clearing in a dense forest of very tall trees. Time seemed to pass slowly. Every now and then a wolf howled. The ECK Master pointed to a great pile of logs lying nearby, ready to be chopped into firewood. Waving his hand gently, he indicated that I was to proceed.

The task was hard. The ax was heavy and kept lodging in the wood. It took a considerable effort to pry the ax head free every time it happened. There must be a better way, I figured.

That was the test.

From a remark Paul had made earlier, I knew this challenge was related to my experience on the racetrack. Then my intuition presented a bright new idea: Begin at the end. This sounded fine but what exactly was I to *do?*

The job progressed as slowly as before. What could be the secret to applying this principle? I mused.

Suddenly the scene disappeared, and I was in a large, tastefully decorated room with the Mahanta, Wah Z. He wore a cream-colored business suit and sat at a desk, his hands clasped in front of him like a TV commentator.

He greeted me cordially and asked if anything was the matter. With an air of hope, I explained the difficulty I was having with the wood-chopping test. I told him that I felt the solution was tied in with the spiritual principle "Begin at the end."

The Mahanta paused a moment. Then he asked, "And how would you *feel*?" emphasizing the last word.

"I'd feel pretty good—there would be no problem!" I returned.

The Mahanta smiled.

68. Spiritual Marriage

For several months a quotation by Paul Twitchell kept coming to mind. It usually arrived out of the blue when I was thinking about nothing in particular. Suddenly it would be there. Each time it brought an upliftment in consciousness.

The quotation was "It is this great force which gives him life. It is God who allows him to survive."

This began recurring so often that I began to wonder. Was the ECK giving me a very specific message? It seemed to fit with certain changes that were taking place in my life.

One lunchtime I was crossing the street when the quotation popped into my mind again. With this, I asked the Mahanta for deeper insight. What was there for me to learn here?

"Look to your right," the Master replied.

At that moment a young bride came through the open doorway of a shop. She was clad in a beautiful gown of snowy white, carrying a bouquet in her joined hands. She was radiant, her cheeks glowing pink with happiness. And she was alone.

Her sense of union and expectancy were so evident

in her solitary pose. The Mahanta was reminding
me of the spiritual marriage: Soul's goal in life—
union with the ECK.

Chapter Ten

The Great Wall

69. Preparing

I sat down with my mother one Sunday afternoon to go over her family history. I explained that I wanted the details that would be lost if she were to depart. "After all," I said, "we might not get an opportunity like this again."

A few weeks later I became conscious that we had no recent photographs of her so I paid her another visit. While she posed by the kitchen window, I readied the camera. An inner voice quietly told me, "Take your time, Robert. You won't get this opportunity again."

Taken aback, I paused. "Why are you taking so long?" my mother asked. "What's the matter?"

"Oh, nothing," I replied.

Less than three days later she was detained at the hospital after a routine checkup. The doctor had detected signs of a long-standing disease.

That night I had a dream. The Dream Master said my mother was nearing the end of another "short story," a lifetime. But he said that the Sound and the Light were with her. When I awoke, I recorded the dream and pondered its meaning. My mother was soon to translate, to pass from this life.

The Dream Master was telling me that for the past few years my mother had enjoyed the spiritual blessing of the Sound Current. The audible aspect of the Holy Spirit and the Light had illuminated her inner life.

This gentle dream message proved an invaluable support to me as events unfolded. It would be several weeks before the doctors completed their tests and could speak with confidence about her true medical condition.

But because of my forewarning, I did not suffer any anxiety over whether or not she would soon pass away. Knowing her destiny, I could relax and accept it.

I saw how the Mahanta works with those close to us, protecting family members and dependents in subtle, unseen ways.

70. Reassignment

For years I had worn a woolly walking hat in the winter months. My mother disliked it, and she made frequent unflattering comments about it. She thought I could surely find something more appropriate for a government official. Finally I gave in and got a decent hat.

A few months later she lay on her deathbed. Her condition was deteriorating rapidly. In her weakened state she had contracted double pneumonia and was unable to speak. The very best she could manage was an occasional whisper. This took considerable effort, so we encouraged her to keep silent. Words weren't necessary.

A couple of days before her death, we all sat by her bedside. For a little diversion I put on my proper hat. She immediately perked up and said, "Did you get rid of that old hat?" The family members looked at each other in amazement, not knowing where she got the strength.

Not long after, she fell into a coma and was not expected to live much longer. At about 10:45 p.m. I saw her briefly in my inner vision. She was clad in radiant white, hovering above the hospital bed. At first I hardly recognized her. She looked so young, about twenty-five instead of sixty-nine. Her hair was a youthful black, glistening in the soft light.

Beside her stood Wah Z, the Mahanta, in a glowing white robe. I had never seen him like this before. Perhaps he appeared as my mother would have expected him to look at that moment, in more traditional biblical garb.

Two days after her death I met her again in the dream state. She was settling into her temporary home. There was no sense of despondency or regret. While we visited, I noticed a familiar face coming down the road to greet us.

"There's Mrs. Kelly," I said in surprise. I hadn't seen her in twenty years. She wore a prim 1950s green suit.

My mother and Mrs. Kelly had been neighbors when I was born. How fitting, I thought, that they should be neighbors again when my mother was reborn. I wondered where she would end up in her next life. Would it bring her an opportunity to meet the Living ECK Master?

Not long after, while doing a spiritual exercise, the Mahanta brought me to her on the Astral Plane. I could see how well she was handling the transition. Though fairly relaxed, she was eager to press ahead with the next step in her unfoldment. She had hesitated at first when offered a new incarnation but then plucked up courage and stepped across the physical frontier.

During contemplation some weeks later the ECK-Vidya opened again, revealing most of my mother's home address in her new physical incarnation. She was with a moderate Protestant family in another English-speaking country. This was an auspicious incarnation, with an opportunity scheduled in her midteens to meet again with the Living ECK Master.

Later, when I related this story to my wife and my sister, I happened to mention, laughing, that the only part of the address omitted from the message was the street name.

The following week my mother came in a dream, as though to redress an oversight. She proudly announced the name of her street.

"It is a beautiful place," she added.

71. Mr. Moon

During a dream I met Paul Twitchell in a rather unsavory bar. He was wearing a navy sweater. With an elbow resting on the counter, he called me over.

He asked me what I'd have. Hardly knowing what to reply, I smiled politely. "Find a table," he said. "I'll order for you and bring it over."

A short while later he arrived at our table with— of all things—a huge ice-cream sundae. I thought, How am I ever going to get through this? There were globs of ice cream of all different colors, with layers of fruit and syrups. Smiling, Paul urged me on.

I took a spoonful off the top. As soon as I swallowed it, I was in a white, snowy land.

The atmosphere was magical, just like a child's fairy tale. Big, fluffy snowflakes fell gently to the ground. Not far from where we stood was a large pond, iced over. Then a snowman walked by, greeting us in a slow, deep voice. The white landscape was filled with rabbits and deer, badgers and birds—a child's wonderland.

Some gnomes and elves were skating on the other

side of the pond, so we walked around to take a closer look. Though the temperature was low, we didn't feel cold. The gnomes handed me a pair of ice skates and ushered me out onto the ice. I said I didn't know how to skate, but that didn't deter them. As I moved across the ice, the surface of the pond changed from frosty to a glassy sheen, reflecting the sky above.

To my surprise it was easy to skate. I grew bolder with each movement. All the little creatures gathered around to watch. The lights from their enchanting little homes twinkled in the background as dusk settled. It was all so curious and joyful. Later when they took me inside their homes, we were warm and snug; Mr. Moon smiled down through the window, clear and bright.

Afterward I asked Paul why I was given this experience. I was greatly surprised by how enjoyable it all was. The kinds of emotions evoked were long-forgotten ones from my past. I had no worries or cares; all was lightness and innocence.

"We need to go back to the innocence of our childhood from time to time," Paul replied. "This way we don't take the journey of Soul too seriously."

72. Sweet Dreams

Because of my sweet tooth, I had to take care not to eat too many sugary foods. Ordinarily I was able to keep this little mind passion under control, but my discipline was still far from perfect. So the Mahanta had to administer a few additional lessons.

While shopping in the supermarket one Saturday morning, I wandered by a group of candy bins. Just a few won't hurt, I thought, scooping a few sweets into a bag.

As I worked around the house that weekend, I passed the candy bag often. Each time, I popped a few more sweets into my mouth—after all, I thought, a few won't hurt.

That night I had a dream where I was a tree, standing in our back garden, clothed in beautiful green foliage. Rosy red apples hung from my short branches; I was well pleased with my lovely attire.

Then I got a shock. From out of the healthy foliage peered a brown rat. Then another. This was dreadful. I hardly knew what to do. Maybe I could knock them off. But how? I called to my wife in the kitchen to get a broom, but she couldn't hear me. Helpless, I awoke with a start.

The meaning was clear to me. I immediately got the candy bag and threw it into the trash can.

The lovely, green, fruit-bearing foliage in the dream was my healthy body. The rats signified disease and infestation. Filling my body with sugars was, effectively, poisoning it.

Presumably the lesson had been well learned. But some weeks later on Christmas Day I had a few glasses of sugared soft drink. Later in the day while playing board games I absentmindedly ate a couple of chocolates. Then a few more. Toward the end of the day I knew I had been careless. That it was a festive occasion made no difference to my body.

Right on schedule, that night I had another dream. I was with some friends when a large white rat came up to me and bit my right index finger. This really hurt. After I had recovered, the same thing happened again. The two bites were very painful and left me shaken.

My dream related to the previous one. The two bites were in response to my two lapses in self-discipline.

Later in contemplation I thanked the Mahanta for giving me this valuable lesson. There was only one thing that puzzled me. Why was the rat white?

Wah Z replied humorously, "Christmas rat!"

73. Puffing Billy

Life had been weighing me down. Everything seemed like such an effort. Though I tried to figure out what had been causing the condition, I got nowhere.

A few nights later during a spiritual exercise the answer came.

I found myself in a cornfield that stretched for miles. To my left in the far distance stood a range of blue-and-gray hills. To my right, much closer, I saw a wood of tall trees where crows cawed noisily and circled overhead. The scene was idyllic.

There was a scarecrow directly in front of me; he was old but still standing. He just leaned forward a little, facing in my direction, motionless.

Next I found myself in a wide, spacious setting. Everything was a pale cream color; the whole area looked and felt so vast and empty that I could have been outdoors. Then I sensed someone approaching.

It was the Mahanta, walking toward me with a bucket of white paint in his left hand. He was wearing a pair of faded blue overalls. Smiling he asked if I could see what stood next to me.

"I can see nothing."

"Here, use these," he said, handing me the paint and a big brush.

Dipping the brush into the white paint I began an up-and-down painting motion in the air, feeling like a mime. To my surprise, an almost intangible surface seemed to hold the paint as the brush glided silently through the air. Gradually a shape began to form.

"It's an old steam locomotive," I exclaimed.

"What was the name often given to it?" the Master quizzed me.

"Puffing Billy!" I replied. The belching plumes of steam and smoke the old locomotives coughed forth had covered the countryside near our home when I was growing up.

"You're like the Puffing Billy," Wah Z said. "You make a huge expenditure of energy and effort to achieve simple ends. Not enough economy. Think of the eagle, how graciously it soars at a great height, wheeling effortlessly in grand arcs across the broad space of heaven.

"With searing acuity it sees all below, even to the smallest detail. There is an economy, a refinement in its motion as it works with the wind and thermals to maintain itself at great height with a minimum of effort."

From the way the Mahanta looked at the Puffing Billy, I knew I had used far too much effort lately to be called an eagle.

"Soul lives by loving," he added. "It loves because it is natural for It to do so. Love is Soul's nature. There is no effort in this, just the joy and grace of being."

194

The Mahanta finished. Glowing with a soft light, he gradually receded from my vision. With that I was back in the cornfield, facing the old scarecrow.

Looking at him I realized that he was actually quite busy at his job. There was not a single crow to be seen in the cornfields. Reflecting on the Mahanta's words, I gazed at the scarecrow and marveled at how well he achieved his objective—with total economy.

74. The Great Wall

At 1:30 in the morning on September 14, 1989, the Mahanta roused me from sleep to record the following inner experience.

I had been put through a series of tests by the Inner Master at a Temple of Golden Wisdom. I felt sure I had met this particular battery of tests before, but I couldn't quite remember them. The tests weren't easy for me; the final one being especially hard because it embodied some of the elements of the tests before it. But somehow I got through them all.

Still at the Wisdom Temple, Wah Z then instructed me to go to a certain room and contemplate. During contemplation I found myself alone in a large cavern. Before me was a huge wall. This was all faintly familiar.

I sat there in the semidarkness for several hours, facing the great wall. I was observing a huge rock that completely blocked the entrance to a vast and wonderful world immediately behind the wall.

I sat totally attentive and in complete silence. I knew the rock would soon begin to roll back, revealing the blinding, unspeakable depths of God.

As I sat there I gradually recalled the two previous occasions when I was confronted with the same opportunity. On each occasion I had panicked as the rock began to move, shouting in terror, "No, God, no! Not yet, not yet!"

This time when the great rock groaned, I was determined to go through with it. Nothing would shake my resolve; I was ready.

After two or three hours, the rock finally began to roll, and great blinding shafts of light came through the tiny space in the great wall. I was completely calm, totally composed. Nothing could shake me now.

But then I heard some words whispered in the darkness, and I could scarcely believe my ears. They were mine.

"Please, God, I'm not ready yet."

They hung like birds in the air; it seemed impossible that they came from my mouth. Instantly the rock collapsed back into position. I just sat there, amazed that the opportunity had passed.

Chapter Eleven

Opening the Gate

75. Premonition

On April 24, 1988, I had a dream in which the Mahanta both revealed a past life and helped me begin healing it.

In the first part of the dream I was relaxing in a large complex of indoor swimming pools in old Atlantis. Only seventeen years of age, I was full of the joys of life as I played with our family dolphins and some friends.

Plenty of natural light entered the complex through the high, transparent walls and roof. Around the pools were many tropical plants and ornate flowers, which thrived in these ideal indoor conditions.

Noticing that my girlfriend had dived in the vicinity of an underwater outlet, I went down to see what she was doing. I swam leisurely in the direction of the reservoir which fed the complex of pools. Being a strong swimmer, I tried to catch up with her. But she kept going deeper along a channel which seemed to lead nowhere.

The light got dimmer as we swam deeper. I grew a little anxious. If she went any farther we might not be able to turn back. Did she know of another exit?

Then we emerged into a huge dark chamber with no visible outlets. We were trapped. And only then did I realize she had intended to commit suicide by drowning. The deep horror of my predicament struck me—I would drown too.

And I did.

The Mahanta was revealing a tragic and painful past-life experience. As a result of my death in that life, I harbored a deep resentment toward the girl whom I had followed to my doom, although I had no clue as to who she was this time around.

To help unwind the sense of hurt, the Mahanta let me experience the dream again, this time surviving the underwater cavern. Instead of drowning, we rose to the surface, a good forty to fifty feet above, and managed to escape through a small grid in the roof.

Furious, I raced after her. She hid in a crowd, but I pushed my way through. Then I suddenly heard her voice behind me. Just as the dream ended, I recognized her as someone close to me in this lifetime.

The dream had an important dual purpose. First, the Mahanta was gently revealing the basis for a key relationship in this lifetime. By showing me the Soul against whom I unknowingly harbored such deep resentment, he was allowing a spiritual healing to begin.

Second, the dream prepared me for a real-life experience which would finally unlock the problem. This dramatic event occurred only five weeks later on Tenerife in the Canary Islands.

76. Death's Sting

I was slowly recovering from the past twelve months, which included three tests. The first was my severe illness in July 1987. The second test came in September, when it felt as if an explosion had occurred behind my eyes. The third test in the cycle waited until the next year, May 1988.

My wife and I were vacationing on Tenerife in the Canary Islands. At about 4:30 p.m. after a spell of reading, I went with my wife to the hotel swimming pool. She sat well back from the edge, sunbathing, while I made for the quietest corner of the pool. Lost in thought, I eased down into the water—and kept going.

I was completely submerged, my feet still weren't touching bottom, and I had lost my grip on the edge. It had all happened so quickly, I hadn't even been able to take a breath. It took me a few seconds to accept the possibility that I was drowning. It hardly seemed real.

This isn't my time to go, I protested silently. What was up? The blue water above me sparkled brilliantly in the hot sunshine. No air. No sound. The world above was bright and blue while I was drowning.

As I came up for the first time, my head failed to clear the surface. My arms moved rapidly to find a grip on the edge. So much time was passing.

Coming up for the second time, I still couldn't clear the surface. No one seemed to notice that I was having trouble. Finally I called out silently, "Wah Z."

When I came up for the third time, my hand just managed to touch the edge of the pool. Kicking hard, I broke the surface of the water. My wife had begun to wonder what all the commotion was about and came across to peer down at me.

"Are you OK?" she asked. I clung to the side and explained what had happened.

Funny, but I felt marvelous. The dream-state preparation on April 24 made all the difference: I hadn't panicked. This had saved me, giving me the presence of mind to call the Mahanta. An old past-life fear had been dissolved.

We like to think that when we've entered the Fifth Circle of initiation that we're home free. Perhaps this is true in a sense, but it only becomes truth through an unremitting process of purification.

77. Coffins

During my contemplation one evening, the ECK Master Fubbi Quantz stepped quietly into my vision. Walking with a slow but purposeful stride he led me to a secluded zone somewhere on the Causal Plane. There was obviously something he wanted to show me. Sensing it was an important moment, I remained silent.

A peculiar sight greeted me. An endless row of open coffins stretched far into the distance. For a moment, I was unsure what to make of this most unusual scene.

"This is your past," the ECK Master explained.

Fubbi Quantz was showing me the extent of my previous incarnations. The corpses on display were duplicates of the various bodies I had used in each of my past lives. Arranged in chronological order, they were quite a spectacle.

The bodies seemed without number. Most of the recent ones were male. Clad in the garments appropriate to each lifetime, they held in their hands the tools and implements I had used each time to make a living.

This short Soul Travel adventure was a vivid reminder of the huge investment each person alive today has already made in their spiritual unfoldment.

78. Mansion of Consciousness

One night I felt inwardly tired. My spiritual exercises had been somewhat uneventful of late. I wondered if there was anything the Mahanta could do to help me shake off this unusual lethargy.

When I entered contemplation that evening, I found myself in a frozen, immobile state, like a statue. Only my eyes could move. Through the thick crust that enveloped my head I could just make out the familiar form of an ECK Master I had seen before. He peered in at me and grunted, "This is a job for Wah Z!"

The Mahanta came on the scene, wearing a light shirt and slacks. Using a hammer and chisel, he began working away at the thick crust of indolence that locked me in. At first little seemed to be happening, then a few cracks appeared. With a sudden rumble, great lumps began to fall away. Now I could move easily and see clearly. The light was dazzling.

Wah Z gave me a few moments to adjust before stepping back and motioning me to follow him.

The Mahanta walked down a white corridor with a high ceiling. We entered a room, spacious and empty, without furnishings of any kind. It gave the appearance of having just been constructed. Bits of plaster and dried drops of paint were speckled here and there on the bare wooden floor. The acoustics in the room were good: the sound of our footsteps echoed softly.

Wah Z pointed silently to the large clear window which admitted plenty of bright morning sunlight. From the garden we could hear the sweetest birdsong.

He led me into the next room. It, too, was unfurnished, with high white walls and a bare wooden floor. The window here also was large, giving the room a fresh, inviting appearance.

As I ambled along behind him, I asked Wah Z, "What is this place?"

He stopped, turned around, and looked at me for a moment. Then he said, "This is your consciousness."

Pausing, he gave me a little time to absorb the implication of what he had just said. "This is your consciousness. These rooms have just been constructed, added on to the vast mansion that expresses your entire journey in these lower worlds." He paused again.

In a sense these rooms were an expression of me, a reflection of my existing state of consciousness, my current level of unfoldment. They were larger, brighter, and more spacious than ever before, letting in more of the Light and Sound of God.

"Then, all of my old states of consciousness must be in some other part of this vast building," I said.

"Yes," he replied, "but they are small and cramped; rooms you would no longer be comfortable entering. We'll let them be."

Walking some more, we returned to the first room. This time one wall was completely decorated and a chair sat in the corner. I also noticed that the room carried the feeling that work was in progress. But where were the workmen? Seeing my curiosity, the Mahanta let me wander into a few nearby rooms to find them, but I came across nobody.

When I returned he smiled: "Have you figured it out yet?"

I frowned a little, feeling unsure. Then I noticed that all of the walls of this first room were decorated and a few additional pieces of furniture were arranged around the room. Seeing my puzzlement, Wah Z spoke: "Your consciousness is shaping and forming your reality all the time. Everything in this room, down to the drops of paint on the floor, you have placed here yourself." I nodded in bewilderment as I detected a faint tang in the air, the smell of a freshly laid carpet.

Smiling and bemused, I looked across at the Master and asked, "Are you real?" He laughed softly and walked over to me. Placing his hand on my left shoulder he said, "Let's have a cup of tea."

79. The Bridge

Business meetings at work were leaving me edgy and ill at ease. I was disturbed to find I couldn't muster the same composure that I enjoyed with ECK activities. What was the secret, I wondered, to carrying the same sense of serenity?

In contemplation, the Inner Master gave me a lovely piece of advice. "During the meeting," he suggested, "ask yourself from time to time, 'What can I do to bring the ECK to these people?'"

I tried this the next day. To my surprise, it worked! It became an effective bridge to close the artificial gap I was creating in my life between ECK activities and the compulsory, mundane chores of the business world.

80. Untying Knots

I was wrestling once again with an old problem, trying to figure out its cause. After numerous attempts to figure out the situation, I asked in contemplation if the ECK could shed some light on my predicament.

Wah Z took me to meet an old ECK Master in a small fishing village on the Mediterranean. His white robe contrasted with his deeply burnished complexion. While the sun burned overhead, he sat quietly mending his net in the shade of a tall tree. His blue eyes followed the needle, guided by his nimble fingers.

Sitting next to the silent ECK Master, watching him busily engaged in his livelihood, I felt a little unoccupied. Sensing this, he rested his hands in his lap and looked across at me. He smiled very softly, then handed me a small object.

It seemed like a lump of pumice. I examined it more closely and found that it was actually a piece of coral. Around it the ECK Master had tightly knotted a slender blue ribbon.

"Untie the knot," he told me.

The knot unraveled easily enough, despite the care it must have taken to tie it correctly.

"That was easy, wasn't it? Now untie the other knot."

"What knot, Master?" I asked, puzzled.

"Look closely; look very closely."

Through the small holes in the coral, I could just make out a trace of blue here and there. Peering closer still, I spied a tiny knot. I smiled up at the ECK Master.

"That one is not so easy," he said. "The ribbon was once outside the coral, but as a living organism beneath the sea, the coral grew around it, calcifying, and enduring only as a dead skeleton. The ribbon is now within the coral. To untie the knot, you must either wear down the coral or crack it open.

"This is how it is with mental habits and negative thinking. They are the root cause of old problems, letting them endure in the subconscious where they can continue to bother the chela for years. To tackle such problems, you must first tackle the underlying structure—the habit. Wear it down or crack it open, but one way or another you must tackle the habit if you are to untie the knot."

With that, he quietly resumed the silent task of mending his net.

81. The River

While on a Soul Travel journey somewhere in the inner worlds I came to a wharf beside a grand, expansive river. An ECK Master was preparing to set sail in a well-trimmed riverboat with a group of tourists. Seeing me on the wharf, he waved and beckoned me to join him at the wheel. I was delighted with the invitation and hopped on board.

The passengers were seated in pious rows along either side of the vessel. Prim and reserved, they looked more like staid schoolteachers than tourists about to set off on an interesting journey along the river. This puzzled me at the time, and I remarked on it to the riverman.

We traveled downriver for about an hour. Then the ECK Master turned the boat around, and we sailed slowly back to our point of departure.

As we traveled, the riverman pointed out the sights along the river. He gave a thoughtful commentary on each while he steered the vessel carefully through shoals and reefs. Oddly the passengers were totally impassive. There was so little response I wondered why the ECK Master bothered.

When we docked back at the wharf and the passengers were stiffly disembarking, I asked him why he did this job, day after day. His reply was a revelation.

"It's worth it," he said. "Even if it takes a long time, someday they will realize it is not the sights that matter, but the river."

82. God-Realization

During my contemplation one day, the ECK Master Paul Twitchell called me into the kitchen. Walking through the swinging door, I found him busy at the sink with a pile of plates, cookware, and drinking glasses stacked beside him. He was washing, so I offered to dry.

Starting with the glasses, I dried with enthusiasm. The ECK Master looked a little funny in his apron, but I said nothing. Concentrating on the task at hand, we worked away in silence.

Through the window I could see two little children playing in the garden, a boy on his bicycle and a girl on her swing. As I dried the glasses to a sparkling sheen, I watched the children's happy movements. At length, Paul looked out and in a reflective tone asked, "If that boy were God-Realized, would he bicycle any differently?"

Since we had not spoken until now, the ECK Master's question seemed to come from nowhere.

"No, Paul, I guess he wouldn't."

Paul got back to washing some more dishes. A few minutes later he looked up again and asked, "If that girl were God-Realized, would she swing any differently?"

"Ah, I suppose not," I replied, looking across at the girl on her swing.

There was a longer pause now as the ECK Master resumed his task of scrubbing each pot thoroughly. I had just finished the glasses and was about to start on the plates. Paul picked up a stainless-steel eggcup and held it to the light. "If you had never seen an egg before, would you have known what this was?" he asked.

I took my time in answering. Paul smiled.

"No, I guess I wouldn't," I finally said.

This discourse delighted me at the time. The Master didn't talk on and on about God-Realization. There were no metaphysical gymnastics, no esoteric terms or profound statements. By gently pondering the simple events in that kitchen, I came to an understanding of what Paul was getting at.

The human mind has a thousand and one fanciful notions of what a God-Realized person should be. Only through actual life experiences can we come to know what this exalted state might possibly mean for each of us.

Chapter Twelve

Wee Two, We Four

83. Past Lives Remembered

In 1979, two years before I began dating Emily, I had a past-life experience in contemplation which affected me deeply. I wrote the following:

> I lived in a small village in China some five thousand years ago. My wife, Tow-Kai-Ay, and I had two lovely daughters, aged fourteen and seventeen. They were called Lo Ti, which meant rising moon, and Si-Chien, the little flower of the blue gentian which was a herb used for medicinal purposes.
>
> We had nothing but each other. Our daughters were the light and joy of our lives, the center of our universe. One day a marauding army invaded our village and wreaked havoc, killing many of the men and raping or abducting the women and girls.
>
> Our two daughters were taken from us. We never saw them again. Our grief was boundless, and we lived out the remainder of that lifetime in the deepest sorrow and loneliness.

Old and forgotten emotions welled up inside me when I had this experience, and I became quite upset. During the ten years that followed, this emotional pain erupted whenever I recalled this tragic event. I had been shown several other painful past-life experiences, but none had this effect. The Chinese recollection stood apart.

I knew at the time that I'd need to refer to it again, but I had no idea why the Mahanta had revealed this particular past life.

84. A Special Date

March 27—the day after we got married—became a special day for Emily and me. It was on this day that the ECK-Vidya revealed to us that we would be late in having a family, perhaps by eight to ten years. We were driving in a remote part of the countryside, a quiet, peaceful setting after the buzz of activity the previous day. My wife proposed that we visit an old castle.

Driving up to the castle, we came upon two pheasants, a male and a female. Oddly enough the noise of the car didn't seem to bother them. Instead of flying off, they stood resolutely in front of our car and refused to budge.

To me this meant our marriage would endure.

After that experience, we decided to explore the area and pulled up by a large field. Strolling across the meadow, we chanced upon another old castle. Coming closer, I noticed the silhouette of an animal standing in an upstairs window. It was a huge, old goat, her great yellow eyes peering down in mesmerizing silence.

At the foot of the castle wall I found the remains

of a kid, stillborn. Perhaps this accounted for the she-goat's frozen, sorrowful pose. Following an inner nudge, I stepped back from the wall for a better look at the mournful creature on her perch high above. This time, from a fresh angle, I got a lovely surprise. Tottering close to its mother, only inches high, was a tiny kid.

It seemed that we would go many years without a family, but in the fullness of time we would have children. Wanting a little more detail I asked inwardly, "How long exactly?" The Master's silent voice replied, "Eight years, perhaps ten."

So, after nearly eight years of marriage, my wife and I were without children. Medical tests had ruled out the possibility. So we were advised by our doctor to adopt. But where? There were no babies for adoption in our own country, nor was there an established framework for adoption from outside the country.

Having let this run for a couple of years, we got a very strong urge in December 1989 to act immediately. By January 1990 I had begun to research the whole subject of foreign adoption, including eligibility, the reliability of adoption agents, legal documentation, health considerations, and other aspects.

During this time I had an experience with another past life. As a troubadour in Moorish Spain during the thirteenth century, I traveled the length of the country every few years to the region of Provence in southern France. Through my song and stories, I directed my talents to the upliftment of the village folk.

A tall, restless fellow, I fell secretly in love with

a young novitiate nun, and she bore a child. However, the thirst for travel and the wandering life drew me on. Our love child was quietly adopted, and my sweetheart took her final vows.

When the question of adoption arose again, I related my Spanish past-life experience to my wife. She understood immediately: she had been the young nun.

85. The Search Begins

We had always intended to adopt two children, both girls. But we didn't want to adopt them both at the same time. One day in January I asked my wife out of the blue, "What if we're offered twins?" She was a bit taken aback by this.

During that same month she had a dream. A lovely fair-haired infant sat in a stroller beneath a transparent canopy. She knew the infant was waiting for a telephone call from us. But it wasn't possible to make the call. Intuitively she knew the child was destined for another.

When she awoke and related the dream to me, we both knew we weren't meant to adopt in Rumania, despite the fact that we already had two reliable contacts there. The fall of communism in that country had opened up many opportunities for adoption.

We wanted to adopt one child, then return a year later to adopt a second. We felt intuitively that both children would be Latin American, not European. The reasons for this were hard to explain, particularly at a time when many people were adopting children from Rumania.

We could only explain to our family and friends that our inner guidance was drawing us in a different direction. This guidance came in dreams, insights, and other spiritual indicators. It was so strong at times that I wondered if the ECK had something extra special in store for us.

86. Another Chance

While I often received a visual outline of certain past lives, my wife was guided mostly by her intuition. She felt that one key piece of the adoption puzzle was still unanswered: What special contribution was she destined to make to our children's unfoldment in this lifetime?

Then in a dream she met two little girls, ten months old. In the dream she was taking a look at their past lives. To her great surprise, one of the girls made a dramatic statement.

"You don't love me!" the little girl exclaimed in a deeply serious tone.

My wife was very shaken by this and replied, "Oh, my dearest, I love you very, very much."

There was a short pause, when the girl replied, "Well, I hope you do a better job this time than you did last time!"

Through the voice of this tiny child, the ECK was saying: This is your golden opportunity to redress errors of the past.

87. The Cat and I

During February I had a dream in which I attended a large garden party. It was hosted by some of my wife's relatives. The great garden at their old country home was alive with my contented in-laws enjoying a good time in the afternoon sunshine.

During the party a cat appeared on the scene. She walked easily through the throng, attracting a lot of attention and loving caresses. Very gradually she made her way toward me and jumped into my arms.

Plainly, I was the one she had chosen to visit. As evening approached, everyone expected the cat to depart, but she didn't budge.

As the light faded, only the cat and I remained.

Almost five months prior to this dream, an elderly aunt on my wife's side had translated. Since the dream took place at her old house, I knew she was letting me know she was returning to earth again to be with us. Why did she appear as a cat? Two reasons: Her name had been Katty, and a cat has more than one life.

88. Sweeping the Path Clean

As March approached, I felt the need to do everything possible, both on the outer and inner, to help along the process of adoption. I was experiencing an acute sense of urgency. My emotional sensitivity was heightened to such a degree that the slightest thought of adoption was extremely painful to me.

It wasn't clear why the ECK had brought this about. I could only alleviate my discomfort by pouring all my energy into locating "our" children. I left no stone unturned. I followed up every conceivable lead without any delay.

We sensed that something of great importance was happening behind the scenes. This conviction was strongly reinforced by a remarkable inner experience.

I had read in *The Living Word* by Sri Harold Klemp, the Living ECK Master, of an effective technique for smoothing out one's course in life. It was important, however, to make no attempt whatsoever to interfere with the freedom of another individual.

First, we sang HU, the sacred name of God. Next

we clearly visualized where we were and where we wanted to be. Then we visualized a giant broom sweeping away all obstacles between the two locations or situations.

Since we were encountering numerous obstacles in our attempts to adopt, I was keen to apply this technique. The first time I tried it, I got a wonderful surprise, something I never expected.

Sitting alone in our bedroom, I sang HU. Then I visualized the little girl we hoped to adopt. Using the giant broom, I swept away the jumble of obstacles between us. As I did this, I distinctly heard *two* little girls calling in warm expectation, "Daddy! Daddy!"

With a start I scrambled back to normal awareness! The sound of their voices packed a powerful emotional wallop and opened my eyes to a whole new dimension.

The ECK seemed to be saying that the second little girl, whom we had planned to adopt the following year, was also being made ready.

89. Gift of Light

After several months of delays we finally got the break we were looking for. Following up a promising referral, we called the foreign adoption agency and got through immediately. The official told us that an infant girl had been placed with them only a few hours ago. They handled eight or so adoptions a year. Did we want to adopt this child?

Given our slow progress to date, this was a bolt from the blue. What should I say? The Mahanta quietly reassured me that it was OK to accept. With the certainty that this little Soul was destined to find us, we agreed.

Wah Z nudged me to ask the child's date of birth. "March 27," the woman replied. That special date again.

There was still a nagging sense inside me that something was missing. Neither of us could quite put a finger on it. For several days, I thought about it, then to help put my heart at rest, I did a variation of the Shariyat technique given by the Living ECK Master.

This simple but highly effective technique goes like this: Formulate a question about the problem that is bothering you, then open at random either book of *The Shariyat-Ki-Sugmad* and read a paragraph. Then chant HU about eight times and contemplate for five minutes. Chant HU eight more times, then continue your quiet contemplation of the paragraph. Then open the book at random again, and read another paragraph.

The relationship between the two paragraphs carries the solution to one's problem in seed form. Sometimes a little extra contemplation, perhaps over the following day or two, will be needed to fully unfold the meaning conveyed by *The Shariyat*. It is also possible to use another book authored by the Living ECK Master instead of *The Shariyat*, as I did on this occasion.

My question was, Should we travel abroad to adopt this child? I picked up *The Living Word* by Harold Klemp and opened it at random. Only an illustration was on the page, a man dressed in western style but in a foreign location. Judging from his pose, I felt he was looking for something dear to his heart.

This simple message helped reassure me that everything was proceeding as it should.

The following morning, May 10, I was awakened at 5:10 a.m. by the telephone. Still half asleep I went to see who it could be. Our lawyer overseas was calling with important news: our adoptive daughter had a twin sister! Not wishing to separate the two girls, the natural mother had decided to place her second child up for adoption also.

The shock could hardly have been greater. Memories of my past life in China came flooding back. Our two lovely daughters were returning, peering across the abyss of time and space directly into our home.

The emotions of this moment wrenched me so deeply that I wept. It hardly seemed possible that something so painful, so far into the past, should finally begin to heal.

The Mahanta smiled softly but did not speak.

My wife, too, was in awe of the extraordinary event that was now unfolding. The natural parents had given the girls names which meant "light." And of course they both had the same birthday, March 27, our special date.

90. Signs from the Holy Spirit

On May 17, a week after we had agreed to adopt the twins, I was walking along a busy street to my office. As I approached the pedestrian crossing, I put the following question to the Mahanta: "Will the adoption be for the benefit and spiritual growth of both girls?"

With that, I stood and waited for the light to change. At that moment, a car approached with the passenger door wide open, even as it turned the corner and swung past me. Realizing what had happened, the driver pulled in by the sidewalk. As she did, I noticed a student driver's notice (an *L* for "learner") on the rear window.

It appeared the Mahanta was saying, "The door of opportunity is open." The turning of a corner indicated the big change of direction coming into our lives, while the L was confirming that we would all learn from the experience. In short the ECK seemed to be saying, "Yes!"

Later that same day during my lunch break, I was again walking along a busy street and thinking about the adoption. I asked the Mahanta to confirm that we were specifically to adopt twins.

As soon as I had formulated the question, a car pulled over right next to me. A woman got out and proceeded to open a baby stroller on the sidewalk. She then lifted her two little infants from the car and tucked them into the stroller seats. They were identical twins.

I could hardly have received a more emphatic reply.

91. Congratulations!

My wife had a similar extraordinary experience with the ECK-Vidya two days later.

She had gone to visit her elderly father who suffered from Alzheimer's disease and needed full-time professional care. It had been impossible to communicate with him for over a year. But she went regularly to keep him company and hold his hand.

As soon as she entered the room on May 19, his face lit up. "Congratulations!" he exclaimed suddenly.

Then he slumped back into his customary, inarticulate pose and never spoke again, either during that visit or at any time subsequently.

92. Good Choice

My wife was wondering how the mother of our twin girls must feel. What was it like to be in a situation where the only course open to you was to place your two lovely daughters up for adoption?

The Mahanta replied to her concern via an unusual outer encounter.

While on her way to visit her father in the hospital one afternoon, she paused to rest awhile on a seat in the public corridor. A large woman sat next to her. Bit by bit, they got into a conversation.

The woman told her that she had placed her only child for adoption some twenty years earlier. Through a toothy grin, she laughed and joked as she told her story. Her openness greatly surprised my wife. The woman had no inhibitions about telling a complete stranger the intimate details to a private side of her life.

Though she was white, her son, whom she had placed for adoption, had a nonwhite father. Unmarried, she knew she was in no position at that time to give him a suitable home. She was very glad to find a safe alternative. She had no regrets.

This encounter gave my wife a whole new perspective. The Golden-tongued Wisdom was telling her that adoption could be a fulfilling and satisfactory choice for the natural mother, not just a painful episode.

93. Que Será, Será

On a sunny morning in June, I was making one of our many visits to our lawyer, while pondering the question, Would my wife and I be able to handle the karmic conditions brought by the adoption? Whatever happened, we wanted to give our children the best possible start in life. I put this question to Wah Z.

He replied easily, "Take things as they come, Robert, and whatever will be, will be."

What happened next was one of those extraordinary events that cause the heart to soar. Just as I was about to cross the street, a large group of ten-year-old schoolgirls advanced toward me from the other side. Only seconds after Wah Z's reply, they began to sing with one voice in a loud, melodic chorus:

"Que será, será. Whatever will be, will be."

I just couldn't believe it. Tears filled my eyes, and I hurried on lest anyone notice.

94. Bus Number Eighty-Four

On August 10 we went to get shots against certain tropical diseases. The doctor warned us of the unusually high incidence of hepatitis B in the region where we would be traveling. The babies would have to be tested for this highly contagious and potentially fatal disease. Should the test results prove positive, the adoptions would be impossible.

We were floored by this news. Out of nowhere loomed the possibility that our adoption plans could totally collapse.

All the following week we waited for the test results and went through much doubt and heartache. Everything had been going so well until now. All the signs, both inner and outer, had been very positive. How could it all end?

Just when the pressure was getting too much for us, a reassuring sign occurred on my bus ride home that evening. When the bus, a number 84, was about two miles from my home, a little boy with pronounced Latin features walked up from the rear of the vehicle and sat directly opposite me. Since his mother was white, he was clearly her adopted son. In fact, the boy even looked a little like one of our daughters.

This held my attention, and I watched him carefully.

As our stop approached I prepared to alight, as did the boy. But his mother called him back.

"This isn't our stop," she shouted. "This is an 84A, not an 84. The 84A will go right by our front door."

Just when it appeared to us as if our two adoptive daughters would remain caught on the Wheel of the Eighty-Four, the cycle of birth and rebirth, this experience showed me that they too were destined to travel all the way to our front door.

I got off the bus in a daze.

95. Across the Water

These gentle messages from the ECK were allaying most of my unease, yet doubt still crept in. Now we worried about the journey the girls would have to make across the vast, seemingly endless ocean that lay between us. The Mahanta again brought reassurance in an unusual way.

We were due to attend a memorial service for the first anniversary of Aunt Katty's death. Before setting off, I told my wife I had a nudge: The Mahanta would give us one final assurance about the adoption.

We walked into the church and took our places in the front pew. Then we noticed the first sign from the ECK: The two altar boys seated before us were identical twins.

The priest began to speak, but something was wrong. He was mumbling in an incoherent, incomprehensible voice, quite impossible to understand. Occasionally a clear word or phrase arose from the chaos. Otherwise everything he said was a complete jumble.

Judging by what was happening, I despaired of the ECK getting a message through. Then we got our first cue. A complete phrase jumped out: "Still small voice," said the priest, then went back to mumbling. At this, my ears perked up.

He muttered some more, then another clear phrase emerged: "I adopt you both as my children." My wife and I looked at each other. It seemed the Mahanta was shaking his finger at us, letting us know we had no reason for doubt.

The priest mumbled some more. We followed a few occasional words that let us know he was referring to a biblical story where Jesus walked on water. In the midst of his mumbling, the priest spoke his third and final clear phrase: "I come to you across the water, O you of little faith."

That floored me. Our daughters *would* reach us from across the ocean.

As things turned out, the girls tested negative for hepatitis B. We heard later that that priest was notorious for incomprehensible sermons. And strangely enough I was never able to find any of the biblical quotations that he spoke that afternoon, search as I might.

96. Eagles in ECK

Years before we decided to adopt, a fellow came to our front door selling geographical etchings of maps from around the globe. Though I didn't normally buy this kind of stuff, I purchased one and hung it beside my writing desk.

Over the years I took it down from time to time to ponder its contours and reflect on its significance. One day, while strolling along the beach, I picked up a small piece of serpentine wood, washed smooth and white by the sea.

Bringing it home, I set it on top of the etching. Somehow they went together. But why? "You'll understand someday," promised the Mahanta.

When we located the region where our two daughters had been born, I bought some travel literature and read up on its history. The region was exactly in the center of the etching hanging over my desk! Translated from the native tongue, its name meant "Land of the Snake-Eating Bird."

Then I made the connection between the word *snake* and the serpentine piece of wood. The snake-eating bird is the eagle.

In April 1990 Sri Harold Klemp had given a talk titled "We Come as Eagles, Not as Doves" at the ECK Springtime Seminar in San Francisco, California. The ECK was reminding us that our children would come as eagles. Crossing the ocean would be no problem.

97. Old Friends

For several months I had had a recurring nudge to contact a woman, a widow with whom I had had no communication over the past twelve years. I doubted whether she would even remember me. Her departed husband, a dignified, elderly gentleman, had been very kind to me when I was a teenager.

The inner nudge said, "Drop her a card at Christmas and let her know you have just adopted two infant daughters." But why?

At that time I was also wondering about the most recent incarnations of our second daughter. The ECK-Vidya shed no light on this, and I didn't persist. But during contemplation in late August, the Master placed two distinct images before my Spiritual Eye then merged them into one.

The images were of the old gentleman and our second daughter.

Now everything made sense. The ECK had been giving me the answer all along, in the nudge to contact the woman and tell her about the adoption. This kind old gentleman was returning to join our family.

98. Tests of Fire and Water

When the legal procedures were far enough along, we traveled overseas to complete the formalities there and receive the children into our care. The official handing-over took place on September 17.

When we returned home with the children, our lawyer called one evening to say he had finished putting together his end of the final adoption papers. He was coming to see us that evening with his wife and daughter. My wife and I had been having a discussion that morning about our daughters' religion. Should they be affiliated with an orthodox religion to ease their entrance into our community? Given local conditions, it made sense. But we were also concerned that it might hamper their growth in ECKANKAR.

When the lawyer and his family arrived, he told us he had a present for us. Assuming we were Catholic, he handed us two rosaries blessed in Bethlehem, the birthplace of Christ. With gratitude we accepted these gifts from the heart. It seemed the ECK was telling us to go ahead and follow the conservative direction.

Our visitors had just departed, having completed the signing of the final adoption papers, when the room was illuminated for a moment by a brief flash. Then we heard water running in the bathroom.

Suspicious, I went to investigate. A pipe had burst, the bathroom was half-flooded, and water gushed from the light switch!

Acting quickly, I called for help from the apartment manager, and we soon had everything under control. Our daughters, almost six months old, remained completely serene while this flurry of activity moved about them.

We were transferred to another apartment on the first floor, then sat back and had a good laugh at our latest adventure. Having asked the Mahanta for a sign as to which direction we should take, he gave the most reassuring answer possible: Our daughters were initiated into the First Circle of initiation in ECK. They had undergone the tests of fire and water to receive the Light and Sound of God.

So our marriage of two became a family of four. The seeds sown millennia ago during that fateful lifetime in China had finally come to fruition. The bond of love had overcome all obstacles.

While we had met in twos and threes over the intervening centuries, we had never had a lifetime where we each performed our original roles: myself as father, Emily as mother, and our two lovely girls as daughters. We were given the opportunity in Spain in the thirteenth century but blew the chance.

This time we were more amenable to the gentle guidance of Divine Spirit. Under the love and protection of the Mahanta, the Living ECK Master, the golden opportunity is here once again.

Glossary

Words set in SMALL CAPS are defined elsewhere in this glossary.

ARAHATA. An experienced and qualified teacher for ECKANKAR classes.

CHELA. A spiritual student.

ECK. The Life Force, the Holy Spirit, or Audible Life Current which sustains all life.

ECKANKAR. Religion of the Light and Sound of God. Also known as the Ancient Science of SOUL TRAVEL. A truly spiritual religion for the individual in modern times, known as the secret path to God via dreams and SOUL TRAVEL. The teachings provide a framework for anyone to explore their own spiritual experiences. Established by Paul Twitchell, the modern-day founder, in 1965.

ECK MASTERS. Spiritual Masters who can assist and protect people in their spiritual studies and travels. The ECK Masters are from a long line of God-Realized SOULS who know the responsibility that goes with spiritual freedom.

HU. The secret name for God. The singing of the word HU, pronounced like the word *hue,* is considered a love song to God. It is sung in the ECK Worship Service.

INITIATION. Earned by the ECK member through spiritual unfoldment and service to God. The initiation is a private ceremony in which the individual is linked to the Sound and Light of God.

LIVING ECK MASTER. The title of the spiritual leader of ECKANKAR. His duty is to lead SOULS back to God. The Living ECK Master can assist spiritual students physically as the

259

Outer Master, in the dream state as the Dream Master, and in the spiritual worlds as the Inner Master. Sri Harold Klemp became the Living ECK Master in 1981.

MAHANTA. A title to describe the highest state of God Consciousness on earth, often embodied in the LIVING ECK MASTER. He is the Living Word.

PLANES. The levels of heaven, such as the Astral, Causal, Mental, Etheric, and Soul planes.

SATSANG. A class in which students of ECK study a monthly lesson from ECKANKAR.

THE SHARIYAT-KI-SUGMAD. The sacred scriptures of ECKANKAR. The scriptures are comprised of twelve volumes in the spiritual worlds. The first two were transcribed from the inner PLANES by Paul Twitchell, modern-day founder of ECKANKAR.

SOUL. The True Self. The inner, most sacred part of each person. Soul exists before birth and lives on after the death of the physical body. As a spark of God, Soul can see, know, and perceive all things. It is the creative center of Its own world.

SOUL TRAVEL. The expansion of consciousness. The ability of SOUL to transcend the physical body and travel into the spiritual worlds of God. Soul Travel is taught only by the LIVING ECK MASTER. It helps people unfold spiritually and can provide proof of the existence of God and life after death.

SOUND AND LIGHT OF ECK. The Holy Spirit. The two aspects through which God appears in the lower worlds. People can experience them by looking and listening within themselves and through SOUL TRAVEL.

SPIRITUAL EXERCISES OF ECK. The daily practice of certain techniques to get us in touch with the Light and Sound of God.

SUGMAD. A sacred name for God. SUGMAD is neither masculine nor feminine; IT is the source of all life.

WAH Z. The spiritual name of Sri Harold Klemp. It means the Secret Doctrine. It is his name in the spiritual worlds.

How to Take the Next Step on Your Spiritual Journey

Find your own answers to questions about your past, present, and future through the ancient wisdom of ECKANKAR. Take the next bold step on your spiritual journey.

ECKANKAR can show you why special attention from God is neither random nor only for a few saints. It is for anyone who opens his heart to Divine Spirit, the Light and Sound of God.

Are you looking for the secrets of life and the afterlife? Sri Harold Klemp, today's spiritual leader of ECKANKAR, and Paul Twitchell, its modern-day founder, have written a series of monthly discourses that give unique Spiritual Exercises of ECK. They can lead you in a direct way to God. Those who join ECKANKAR, Religion of the Light and Sound of God, can receive these monthly discourses.

As a Member of ECKANKAR You'll Discover...

1. The most direct route home to God through the ECK teachings on the Light and Sound. Plus the opportunity to gain wisdom, charity, and spiritual freedom in this lifetime through the ECK initiations.

2. The spiritual meaning of dreams, Soul Travel techniques, and ways to establish a personal relationship with Divine Spirit through study of monthly discourses. These discourses are for the entire family. You may study them alone at home or in a class with others.

3. Secrets of self-mastery in a Wisdom Note and articles by the Living ECK Master in the *Mystic World,* a quarterly newsletter. In it are also letters and articles from ECK members around the world.

4. Upcoming ECK seminars and other activities worldwide, new study materials from ECKANKAR, and more, in special mailings. Join the excitement. Have the fulfilling experience of attending major ECK seminars!

5. The joy of the ECK Satsang (discourse study) experience in classes and book discussions. Share spiritual experiences and find answers to your questions about the ECK teachings.

How to Find Out More

To request membership in ECKANKAR using your credit card (or for a free booklet on membership) call (612) 544-0066, weekdays, between 8:00 a.m. and 5:00 p.m., central time. Or write to: ECKANKAR, Att: Information, P.O. Box 27300, Minneapolis, MN 55427 U.S.A.

Introductory Books on ECKANKAR

Cloak of Consciousness,
The Mahanta Transcripts, Book 5
Harold Klemp

Pressured by problems, fears, and life's constant barrage of little irritations, many of us insulate ourselves from the harsh world around us. Harold Klemp, the spiritual leader of ECKANKAR, shares insights to help you replace this cocoon of fears with the mantle of God's love, the cloak of consciousness.

ECKANKAR—Ancient Wisdom for Today

Are you one of the millions who have heard God speak to you through a profound spiritual experience? This introductory book will show you how dreams, Soul Travel, and experiences with past lives are ways God speaks to you. An entertaining, easy-to-read approach to ECKANKAR. Reading this little book can give you new perspectives on your spiritual life.

The Spiritual Exercises of ECK
Harold Klemp

This book is a staircase with 131 steps. It's a special staircase, because you don't have to climb all the steps to get to the top. Each step is a spiritual exercise, a way to help you explore your inner worlds. And what awaits you at the top? The doorway to spiritual freedom, self-mastery, wisdom, and love.

Dreams, A Source of Inner Truth
(Audiocassette)

Dreams are windows into worlds beyond the ordinary. This two-tape set can help you open these windows through insights and spiritual exercises given by Sri Harold Klemp, spiritual leader of ECKANKAR.

For fastest service, phone (612) 544-0066 weekdays between 8 a.m. and 5 p.m., central time, to request books using your credit card, or look under **ECKANKAR** in your phone book for an ECKANKAR Center near you. Or write: **ECKANKAR, Att: Information, P.O. Box 27300, Minneapolis, MN 55427 U.S.A.**

There May Be an
ECKANKAR Study Group near You

ECKANKAR offers a variety of local and international activities for the spiritual seeker. With hundreds of study groups worldwide, ECKANKAR is near you! Many areas have ECKANKAR Centers where you can browse through the books in a quiet, unpressured environment, talk with others who share an interest in this ancient teaching, and attend beginning discussion classes on how to gain the attributes of Soul: wisdom, power, love, and freedom.

Around the world, ECKANKAR study groups offer special one-day or weekend seminars on the basic teachings of ECKANKAR. Check your phone book under **ECKANKAR**, or call **(612) 544-0066** for membership information and the location of the ECKANKAR Center or study group nearest you. Or write **ECKANKAR, Att: Information, P.O. Box 27300, Minneapolis, MN 55427 U.S.A.**

☐ Please send me information on the nearest ECKANKAR discussion or study group in my area.

☐ Please send me more information about membership in ECKANKAR, which includes a twelve-month spiritual study.

Please type or print clearly   940

Name _____

Street _____ **Apt. #** _____

City _____ **State/Prov.** _____

ZIP/Postal Code _____ **Country** _____